HOW TO DIE AND STAY DEAD

Barbara,
It was wonderful meeting you.
Don't grow weary in well doing
for in due season you will
reap, if you
faint not.

Teresa

Teresa S. Johnson

xulon
PRESS

(Books)
>   What the Bible Says to the Minister, Leadership Ministries Worldwide
>   The Discipler's Manual, F.E. Marsh
>   Wycliffe, Dictionary of Christian Ethics, Carl F.H. Henry, Editor
>   Strong's Concordance, James Strong, LL.D., S.T.D.

(Sermon Reference)
>   Rev. Joseph Lyles, Pastor, A Celebration of God's deliverance, 2003

(Quotes)
>   The New National Baptist Hymnal, Special Edition

Cover concept by Ericka Johnson

www.xulonpress.com

For all of you who are tired of being defeated.

Thanks to TBN (Trinity Broadcasting Network) for all the women and men of God who encouraged me tremendously.

A heartfelt thank you to singer, Ron Winans and the family (whom I've never met) for, A Consecrated Song.

Thank you Dr. Buck, of Maple Springs Bible College and Seminary for the Personal Evangelism & Christian Living Class.

Thank you to my Pastor, Joseph W. Lyles of Fort Foote Baptist Church for the many years of teaching and application of the Word of God.

Acknowledgments

First I want to thank my heavenly Father, my creator, from whom I draw all of my strength. Thank you Jesus; it feels so much better to finally know how to bring my flesh under submission and have it remain there.

To my husband Eric, for whom I have an undying love. We journeyed together through many facets of life, and through it all, I am proud to say I could not have asked for a better Soul Mate. To God be the Glory, great things He has done. You're my King.

To my daughter Ericka, truly you are a gift from God. You are always there with open arms waiting to show forth affection, encouragement and love. You have a beautiful Spirit. I love you, sweetheart.

Thank you, Author Crystal Ellis for appearing in my life at a vendor's day out with Angela. You sparked something on the inside of me, and because of that, what had been birthed deep in my spirit was brought forth. Thank you for your support.

Ethel, my best friend, thank you for listening to me pour out my heart for so many years. Thanks for the encouraging words, for being supportive, always being available, and for making me laugh even when I wanted to cry. I pray God will bless you as you have been a blessing to me.

Tameka and Kim, my little sisters. Oh, if I could spare you both from going through anything I went through, I would. You heard the good, the bad, and the ugly. You were always listening. Now finally, here's the end result. May it richly bless you.

Thanks to my parents for training me, for the lessons I've learned and for the unconditional love you have shown me throughout the years.

Special thanks to my sisters and brothers for the closeness we share. I love and appreciate each of you, and I pray for increase in your lives.

Liz Lee, thank you from the bottom of my heart for being real. Your wisdom and godly advice never fell on deaf ear. You are truly a woman of obedience and faith.

Tish, my friend, my mentor, thanks for the push in more ways than one. Thanks for the confidence you have in me. I still laugh and I am honored to have a Pastor as my Friend. God Bless you.

Contents

❧

1

Do you have a Promise?

So put to death the sinful, earthly things lurking within you. Have nothing to do with sexual sin, impurity, lust, and shameful desires. Don't be greedy for the good things of this life, for that is idolatry. God's terrible anger will come upon those who do such things. You used to do them when your life was still part of this world. But now is the time to get rid of anger, rage, malicious behavior, slander, and dirty language. Don't lie to each other, for you have stripped off your old evil nature and all it's wicked deeds. In it's place you have clothed yourselves with a brand-new nature that is continually being renewed as you learn more and more about Christ, who created this new nature within you. (Colossians 3:5-10 NLT)

Firstt let me ask you, ___Do you have a Promise?___ If God has not verbally given you a promise, find a promise in his Word for your situation, circumstance, issue or problem. Ask God to help you find it. After you get that promise, in order for it to come to pass, you have to receive it. **Whatever you ask for in prayer, believe that you have received it, and it will be yours. (Mark 11:24 NIV)** Exercise your faith. **Now faith is the substance of things hoped for, the evidence of things not seen. (Hebrews 11:1 KJV)**

Do you have the faith to believe something that you can't see?

Just as God promised to restore Israel, the very promise was made for you as well. **This is what the Lord says: In the time of my favor I will answer you, and in the day of salvation I will help you. I will keep you and will make you to be a covenant for the people, to restore the land; and to reassign its desolate inheritances to say to the captives, come out, and to those in darkness, Be Free! (Isaiah 49:8-9 NIV)**

Don't you want to be FREE?

When God gives you a promise, He's giving you hope. He is giving you the end result to a situation or thing, and trusting you to endure through the beginning and middle stages. If you know how the story ends, why not persevere to the very end? Would you prefer going through your crisis without a word from God, speaking life into your situation? We can't all say we have a promise from God buried within their hearts. I don't know about you, but I don't think I would have made it without God's promise. I held onto God's word in spite of what things looked like. I held onto the fact that God's Word would not, and could not, return unto Him void. How can you give up on any thing that you know has a positive outcome?

2

Wait on the Lord

**Wait on the Lord: be of good courage, and
he shall strengthen thine heart: wait, I say,
on the Lord. (Psalm 27:14 KJV)**

Marriage is honorable. It's a union ordained by
God. It can be the most beautiful love
connection between two people with many cherish-
ing and precious moments, as well as sacrifices and
challenges. The side affect of marriage taught me
about me, and how to truly trust God.

I endured a lot over the period of my marriage. I
had many sleepless nights. I realize now that half the
emotional roller coasters I went on could have been
avoided. I see how I could have contributed more to
the marriage. There are always two sides to every
story. You each see it differently. As male and
female, you each have different expectations. Come
with me as we journey through my version.

"I remember my affliction and my
wandering, the bitterness and the gall. I
well remember them, and my soul is
downcast within me. Yet this I call to mind
and therefore I have hope: Because of the
Lord's great love we are not consumed,
for his compassion never fail. They are
new every morning; great is your faithfulness. I say to myself, "The Lord is my
portion; therefore I will wait for him."
The Lord is good to those whose hope is in
him, to the one who seeks him; it is good to
wait quietly for the salvation of the Lord."
(Lamentations 3:19-26 NIV)

I suffered long. Some of the suffering was due to
my immaturity. Some was due to my insecurities.
Much was because God wasn't the center of my life.
When God is at the center of your life, it's easier to
cope with things. There's a sense of hope, instead of
feelings of hopelessness.

When I finally reached out to God, I found
myself constantly asking him questions. Seldom did
I hear any answers. As years passed, things that
most concerned me took a turn for the worse. I was
determined to get some answers from God. When
you give God control over your life and affairs,
there's a sense of security. And whether you're in a
crisis or not, you have confidence that you can ask
what you will.

My questions were:

"How long do I have to be in this predicament?

When will you change my circumstances Lord?"

Over time, I screamed and flooded heaven with questions. I got to the point where I had to stop talking and just listen. I thought maybe if I shut up for a minute, I'd hear something. It was hard because I was use to running my mouth constantly to God. I decided to wait for him to tell me something, any thing. Keep in mind, all situations aren't the same. We don't always get the same responses. Your outcome may even be different.

At last, the responses began to come in. They didn't all come at once, but it served the same purpose. I heard some of these responses through others, and some I heard directly.

"My time is not your time" (We don't always get things when we want them, but God's timing is the perfect time).

"Prepare" (There's always a preparation period, just as we prepare to bring a baby home, or make preparations for a marriage, an interview, activities or events, etc. we also have to prepare to receive the things of God).

"De clutter your mind" (You can't hear from God when your mind is busy racing a mile a minute. Your brain is on overload. You're focused on too many things. Most of the things you're dwelling on don't even concern you. Some of the things cluttering your mind, you have no control over, and can do nothing about. A lot of the things that cloud your mind, you know what to do, but refuse to. God is saying, get rid of those things).

"Clean your little garden" (It is important to take

care of your home, and your surroundings. Whether it's cleaning, cooking, spending time with your spouse/children/family, covering them in prayer, taking care of finances, or being a representative of Christ before them, etc.).

"Do what you know to do" (Stay connected to the vine, which is God. Stay in his Word. Don't lose heart. Don't stop Praying. Fellowship with other believers. Practice what you preach).

"Be Steadfast. Don't consider the stumbling, I have forgiven you." (The strong hold that bound you, no longer grips you. God has forgiven you of your sin. It's now a thing of the past. Don't beat yourself up or allow anyone else to. Move forward, continuing to do what's right from this period on. You are a new creature).

"My grace is sufficient for you" (Hold on to your faith, whatever God decides to do about a particular thing, He will sustain you in the process).

"When I do this for you, don't forget about me. Think of ways to give back to the Kingdom." (Financial breakthrough-When God restores you, don't forget about him. Remember, you don't live to eat, you eat to live. A car is just for transportation. Remember that you have to reach out strengthening and helping others).

God will definitely encourage your heart while you wait because during this period, he's teaching you patience. He's teaching you the true meaning of long suffering, and perseverance. He's teaching you how to humble yourself. Sometimes, I just needed direction. I just needed to know I was on the right track or how to get on the right track. I began to lust after any thing God wanted to tell me, whether it was instruction or chastisement. I was yearning for His conversation.

As the heat was turned up in my situation, challenges grew greater, and things sometimes seemed unbearable. I had to make up my mind, **"Lord your word is a lamp for my feet and a light for my path. I've promised it once, and I'll promise again: I will obey your wonderful laws. I have suffered much, O LORD; restore my life again, just as you promised. LORD, accept my grateful thanks and teach me your laws. My life constantly hangs in the balance, but I will not stop obeying your law. The wicked have set their traps for me along your path, but I will not turn from your commandments. Your decrees are my treasure; they are truly my heart's delight. I am determined to keep your principles, even forever, to the very end."(Psalm 119:105-112 NLT)**

You have to determine in your heart to hang in there regardless of how difficult things appear. Your manifestation might not happen over night, but if you stay the course, you will see all kinds of wonderful blessings. God is a God of restoration. He can and will restore your marriage/relationship.

Seeing God clean both you and your mate up is priceless. When you finally start to receive the desires of your heart, and you're experiencing abundance in every area, whether it's (communication, affection, intimacy (undue benevolence), oneness, faithfulness, respect, undying love, peace, being on one accord, being set free and delivered from strongholds, joy, enjoying one another, appreciating one another or simply exercising self-control) that's well worth waiting for. I'm talking about complete restoration that only comes from God. These are some of the rewards you can expect if you trust God and wait patiently.

God can transform people right before your very eyes. When you experience such transformation in your own life, your gratitude deepens, your hunger grows greater, and your witness gets stronger. Transformation brings forth many results. Submission is one. When a person totally submits to God wholeheartedly and makes you second in his or her life (instead of whatever number you use to be) that's a transformation worth waiting for. When a person stands up and calls you blessed, and praises you, that's a transformation worth waiting for. With such transformations, you quickly see that your labor was, and is not in vain after all. But if you don't stay connected to God, you will never see or experience such transformation. So if you're one of those people who want to know, if you wait on the Lord and do what you're suppose to do, what's in it for you, your answer is, Restoration.

I'm sure you know that you can't obtain any of these results successfully without God.

(John 15:5 KJV) says, **I am the vine, ye are the branches: He that abideth in me, and I in him, the same bringeth forth much fruit: for without me ye can do nothing**.

With God at the center of our lives, we can wait

with joy. God's joy is our strength. **But they that wait upon the LORD shall renew their strength; they shall mount up with wings as eagles; they shall run, and not be weary; and they shall walk, and not faint. (Isaiah 40:31 KJV)**

Sometimes the wait can take many years, as it did for me, but don't give up. Oftentimes, God will even change you before He changes the situation, and that's a good thing. Waiting on the Lord brought me contentment and positive outcomes. It wasn't always easy, and sometimes I threw temper tantrums, but that didn't speed up the process any. No matter how I acted, I still had to wait. When I exercised patience, I had to wait. When I grew impatient, I had to wait. But it always felt better when I was patient. Things always worked out a little better when I was patient.

While I was waiting, it seemed like decades were passing me by. But through it all, my breakthrough came at the appropriate time. It's not a good thing to get things before time. There needs to be a receiving position. What do you think would happen if you hired a caterer for a dinner party, and due to unforeseen circumstances, he or she had to deliver the food two days earlier than planned? You weren't prepared to receive all that food. You have to figure out how to keep it fresh. You don't have adequate storing space. Things are becoming chaotic. Now the difference is, when God gives you something, there are no details to iron out. Everything has already been taken into consideration beforehand. You can freely receive what God gives because the time is right.

Now, let me back track for a minute. While I waited, of course there were times when I got restless. I wanted things to happen sooner. But I'm happy to say, I never went back and forth on believing God. Yeah, I tried to rush Him, but never did I doubt what He could or would do. I knew without a doubt the promise would come to pass. My problem was I knew God could change things in the twinkling of an eye, and I expected him to change things in the twinkling of an eye.

If God told me, or if he told someone else to tell me he was going to do something, I wanted it right then and there. I quickly learned that we have to be in position to receive. Through waiting, I learned to appreciate things more, not taking so much for granted. I learned how to use the waiting period to work on myself. All that waiting taught me things that I wouldn't have learned otherwise. It taught me about me, others, life in general, and about God.

One thing is certain, if you wait in the correct manner, you'll bypass the extended process. I believe you'll continue to go through processes until you get it right. Until you get a full understanding of, why you're there, and what you're suppose to get from being there. The more you act out of character and in disobedience, the longer the process.

Whatever you're waiting for, if God has promised it, it shall come to pass. The question is, Are you prepared to receive it? As you wait patiently, allow your soul to truly find rest in God. David said, **"My soul finds rest in God alone; my salvation comes from him. He alone is my rock and my salvation;**

24

he is my fortress, I will never be shaken." (Psalm 62:1-2 NIV)

3

Deny Yourself

❦

You need to deny your flesh. **If any man will come after me, let him deny himself, and take up his cross, and follow me. (Matthew 16:24 KJV)**

We have to decide daily that we're going to do what God wants us to do, say what He tells us to say, and go where He tells us to go. You can't use the excuse that God doesn't talk to you, or you don't hear his voice. He said his sheep know his voice. Aren't you his sheep? You have a responsibility to seek God daily. You need to know who he is. Make time to read his Word daily. Through His word you will hear His voice, and you will learn about him.

Ask God to show you how to not give your flesh what it wants. God has given you the third person of the Trinity, who is, The Holy Spirit. Once you receive Salvation, that Spirit dwells on the inside of you, and He will guide you in rejecting the temptations of your flesh.

I remember I made a vow to God that I would do things his way. **When you make a vow to the LORD your God, be prompt in doing whatever you promised him. For the LORD your God demands that you promptly fulfill all your vows. If you don't, you will be guilty of sin. (Deuteronomy 23:21 NLT)**

I promised I would deny my flesh in specific areas no matter now bad it hurt. I desperately needed a change. Don't be confused, denying yourself doesn't mean you become a doormat, or open to abuse or misuse. Denying yourself means doing God's will, not yours.

Realize you can't base your life on the way others live. This is about living your life as God deems necessary for you. It's about doing what works for you according to God. There's a level of responsibility that you must face. In denying yourself, some things you won't be able to do, say, or participate in. It might not seem fair. It might not even feel good at that time, but if you will commit to living a life that's pleasing to God, your maturity level will increase. You will quickly see that you've been moved into a higher standard of living zone.

God wants us to live a holy lifestyle. We should all strive for holiness. But remember it's a continual process. You're continuously being renewed, day by day. You have been stripped of your old ways. Your habits and deeds have changed. You're no longer interested in the things you use to do. God will give you instruction as you live your life pleasing in His sight.

I made mistakes, but I learned how to not wallow in sin. I made up my mind, when God forgave me of the wrong I did, I wouldn't just say thank you; I would turn from that wrongful act. I made a conscious decision to not do it again. There were things that I struggled with, but I asked God to help me not compromise. I didn't want to let Him down.

I wasn't always obedient. I fell short of God's glory, but God gave me brand-new mercies every day. The same mercy is available to you. As time went on, I saw that the trials, problems, and concerns I faced, were not always about me. Often, they were about the God in me. It was about God being glorified, by any means necessary. Satan wanted to attack the God in me, so he would stir things up, trying to cause confusion. But God, being the awesome, victorious God that he is, always turned what Satan meant for bad around, and God received the glory.

The flesh constantly screams for what it wants. It doesn't concentrate on what's good or bad, just the want. That's why you must **watch and pray so that you will not fall into temptation. The Spirit is willing, but the body weak. (Matthew 26:41 NIV)**

We consider ourselves to be good people, but our goodness isn't what keeps us from falling to temptation. It's God who provides the way of escape for us. It was hard for me to deny my flesh when I was constantly being disappointed, angered, frustrated, or annoyed. But, we all have to finally get to the point where we take a stand against temptation, and not waver. If we're going to serve God, we can't allow people to change who we are. We have to get to a point where others cannot dictate how we live, how we respond to friction, or who we are. The only dictator in our lives should be our heavenly father, our creator, the creator of heaven and earth.

When denying yourself, the tongue would be a good place to start. I had to learn that it's okay to not have the last word, especially if it were argumentative or sarcastic. The majority of time, my words were argumentative and sarcastic. One time I carried on for so long, arguing AT my husband, until I was totally exhausted. When I laid down, the Holy Spirit said, "raving lunatic." At first, I laughed, but then I was embarrassed. No one heard that comment but me, but it sure made me take a long look at myself.

You know the bible says that **a quarrelsome wife is like a constant dripping on a rainy day; restraining her is like restraining the wind or grasping oil with the hand. (Proverbs 27:15-16 NIV)** My husband who rarely ever argued, always said, all he wanted was a little peace and quiet. It's amazing he hung in there with me. I could argue for hours at a time, and by myself. You're talking about pure torture. Nothing was ever resolved by me ranting and raving. If anything, it brought greater distance between us.

I had to learn to stop fussing and start praying more. I had to show God that I trusted Him by listening and obeying him. I had to stop the murmuring, recognizing that it was sin. I had to remember who my commitment was to. Your commitment should be to God, not people. People change. People make errors, but God remains the same yesterday, today and forever.

Stay in God's presence and you will surely die to the improper desires of your flesh. Denying your flesh can actually bring you contentment in so many other ways. It did for me on the job.

• **Job**

I never had contentment on a job until three years ago. I was believing God for one position and He gave me a lesser position. I was told by a Prophet, God knew that position wasn't what I wanted, but it was what he wanted me to have, so find contentment. Contentment didn't come over night. However, God showed me the difference it would have made getting the position I wanted, versus the position He wanted me to have.

Sometimes, what we want isn't always what God wants for us, nor is it what's best for us. If we will just accept what God wants to give us at that time, we will find contentment we never knew. With contentment comes many valuable lessons. When we choose to believe, we are promoted because we're educated, intelligent, or because we're so good at our job, we're taking God out of the equation. We're saying we did all this in our own strength when in fact God has equipped us with skills and knowledge. He has given us the ability to be successful and to expand beyond measure. **For promotion cometh neither from the east, nor from the west, nor from the south. But God is the judge: he putteth down one, and setteth**

up another. (Psalm 75:6-7 KJV)

When you know promotion comes from God, you stop blaming supervisors when you're not promoted. Yeah, supervisors can procrastinate. It may even appear they're holding you back, but ultimately they don't make the final call. Whether they are fond of you or not, if God chooses to promote you, in His time, you will be promoted.

God has good, pleasing, and perfect plans for us. He wants us to be transformed people with renewed minds, living to honor and obey him. He wants only what's best for us. He gave His Son to make our new lives possible, so we should joyfully give ourselves as living sacrifices for His service, even on the job.

4

Are you beginning to get a glimpse of Death?

W hen you've successfully denied yourself, you're not wrestling back and forth in your mind or deed. You're no longer wishy-washy. And you certainly don't hold grudges against people. You're not jealous of what God is doing for others. You've determined in your heart to stand firm, trusting God to work things out for you. **Give all your worries and cares to God, for He cares about what happens to you. (1 Peter 5:7 NLT)** Stop wavering and doubting.

We all have been through unhealthy, unnecessary stress at some point or another. But isn't it time to get rid of the drama? I was one who held things inside because I thought I was keeping the peace. I would allow things to fester, and then like a volcano, I erupted. Once I went into drama queen mode, I was nerve wrecking. Now if I can say that, you know it was pretty bad.

Let me give some tips from personal experience. Just because you don't use profanity or get violent in your moment of outrage, doesn't mean you're not still sinning. I had a way of expressing myself and getting my comments across without vulgar language. What I said was still very negative. It was demeaning and often judgmental. It was sinful.

I'm going to just throw some things out there to consider when denying your flesh. First of all, please respect your body. You don't have to ever throw yourself at anyone sexually. There's more to you than your body. Don't compromise yourself or your values for sex.

Neither should you withhold sex from your SPOUSE as a weapon. Doing so creates problems. It opens the door for the devil, the enemy, to come in. The bible talks about a time of absence that you both agree on, if and when that time is set aside for prayer. Otherwise, don't kid yourself. There are many vultures in disguise out there lusting and waiting to pounce on your lonely, neglected mate. Don't give your mate a lame excuse to prowl or tread on dangerous territory.

Stop giving your mate the silent treatment as punishment. Communication is very essential in any type of relationship. Once communication begins to shut down, it takes Jesus to open those lines back up. It's too dangerous to completely shut down. Some things need to be discussed and in a non argumentative environment. There's a difference between always running off at the mouth (saying every thing on your mind), and choosing to address issues in a positive way, at the right time. God will present the perfect timing when the person will be open to receive and hear your heart's concern.

Don't try to teach your mate a lesson by not cooking or cleaning. Angry or not, you still have to eat, and I heard somewhere that cleanliness was next to godliness. You still have to show love in spite of how you feel. You're supposed to do unto others as you would have them do unto you, not as they do unto you.

Stop focusing on the person getting over all the time. You feel like you're being taken advantage of. You feel you're doing what's right, and he or she is reaping the benefits. (He or she has their cake and they're eating it too) as some say. They even gloat about having a good wife or good husband. Ask yourself a question. Since God sees all and knows all, who is really getting over?

I often hear, and have said, "It's just not fair!" It might not be when you look at things in the natural, but you will never die if your attitude is always geared toward payback. So what do you do? You do unto God! The commandments are His. Once again, you wait on the Lord, realizing that in this world, you shall have tribulation, but you wait being of good cheer because you know God has already overcome the world. If he overcame the world, truly He can help you overcome your obstacles and dilemmas.

God doesn't force Himself on us. If we act as if we can handle our problems on our own, then He will let us try. But why even risk making a bigger mess out of things when God already knows the entire situation, as well as the end result. Why not consult with Him and make life easier?

I encourage you to continue doing what's right in spite of what people around you do. One of my favorite scriptures, **(Galatians 6:9 KJV)** says, **and let us not be weary in well doing: for in due season we shall reap, if we faint not.** So in other words, don't give up. What better way to witness to the world than by denying yourself for the sake of the Kingdom. After all, the kingdom is the ultimate goal, isn't it?

5

The Glory of the Lord

In the morning you will see the glorious presence of the LORD. He has heard your complaints, which are against the LORD and not against us. (Exodus 16:7 NLT)

When you believe that **all things work together for good to them that love God, to them who are the called according to his purpose (Romans 8:28 KJV)**, it's easier to stay focused. When you experience the presence of the Lord in your situation, you quickly come to a place where nothing will distract you to the point of turning back or doubting God.

The bible says, **Greater is He that is in us, than he that is in the world.** This is so true. Knowing that the God in you is greater than the devil in the world keeps you from living in darkness. It keeps you from attempting suicide. It keeps you from contemplating divorce. It keeps you from depression, drugs, alcohol, adultery, bitterness, loneliness, low self-esteem and over indulgence (be it food, spending, etc.).

Knowing that the God in you is greater than the devil in the world also helps you to deal with all the pain, hurt and disappointment in and surrounding your life. We're over comers. We're conquerors. We're victorious, and why? The Holy Spirit is working on the inside of us.

If you pay attention, in the midst of your hurt, God is always there strengthening you and enabling you to reach out to others. When I learned to reach out to others, I didn't have time to throw long drawn out pity parties. I didn't have time to focus on my problems because it appeared God wanted me to encourage others.

Sometimes, I found myself encouraging people with the same concerns as mine. All that meant was, as I ministered to the needs of others, God was ministering to me. He was giving me the same word to apply to my own situation. Isn't that awesome? Reaching out in love guarantees not only enriching the lives of others, but your life will be enriched as well. God doesn't want us to be selfish in our despair. The bottom line is, as long as there is a generation, there will be greater concerns than just ours.

Knowing God lived in me, forced me to want to get to know Him better. It forced me to get in His Word. I began channeling my energy into feeding my spirit, studying to show myself approved. I made deposits, and as a result, I was able to make withdrawals from God. Here's a deposit that you can make, draw close to God, and see won't you experience His glory. You will see him working daily on your behalf.

Don't you want to see his glory?

Speaking of Glory, I have a great appreciation for clouds. They fascinate me. They go from looking like fluffy cotton candy to a large cotton blanket. It's almost as if I could wrap myself in clouds and hide in the sky. Sometimes, when I look at the sky, the clouds are just breathtaking. They're comforting, and God has shown me many things through the clouds.

- **Appointed Time**

A co-worker of mine named Barry had been sick. He had cancer. For months, I interceded in prayer, and cried unexplainable tears for him. I was later told he was getting worse and had been hospitalized again.

Another co-worker was on her way to visit him. She informed me that he was on a ventilator. Well that hadn't quite registered with me unfortunately. I wasn't sure what that meant. But at any rate, God had spoken privately to me. He told me to go to the hospital, lay hands on Barry, anoint his head with oil, and pray the prayer of healing.

I went to the hospital with two co-workers. Once we got there, I wasn't able to go in the room with Barry alone as I would have preferred. I was a little uncomfortable, as I was out of my comfort zone, but I was obedient to God. I anointed his head with oil, prayed, and I believed Barry would be healed. I knew he could hear me, and I felt he gave me his permission to anoint his head and pray.

Moments after I left Barry's room, I heard the family discussing taking him off life support. My thoughts were, whatever they decided, God could overrule. I left the room confidently knowing Barry would be fine. As I walked toward the car to meet my co-workers, I began crying and doubling over. Soon I couldn't take another step. I didn't understand what was going on. I had never experienced this feeling before. Feeling very awkward, I fought to stand up, and I continued walking to the car.

By the time I reached the car, I was crying uncontrollably. I was no longer able to hide the tears from my co-workers. As I tried to catch my breath, I was drawn to look up to the sky. I saw Barry sitting on a cloud with his legs crossed. His hand was resting on his chin. He had a smirk on his face, as he often had in the office when I shared a testimony with him. I couldn't believe it. Before I knew it, I was laughing, and yelling to my co-workers, "Look at Barry!" Of course they couldn't see him. It was the most glorious thing I had ever witnessed, and I praise God for allowing me to see that. Sometimes, God will do special things just for you.

The next day while at my desk, we got the call that Barry had passed. All I could do was moan and groan. Not only was I hurt, but frustrated, because I had faith that God would heal Barry. Later that night, God put a song in my heart, "It is well with my Soul." I searched my hymnal for the complete lyrics:

When peace, like a river, attendeth my way,
When sorrows like sea billows roll;
Whatever my lot, Thou hast taught me to say,
It is well, it is well with my soul.
(H.G. Spafford, P.P. Bliss)

The lyrics truly soothed my heart, and I was at peace. But God didn't stop there. Later, He addressed my deepest, embedded, unexpressed thoughts. Never think God isn't listening. He knows your thoughts afar off. In the back of my mind, for only a split second if that, I asked, "Why would you tell me to go to the hospital if you knew?"

Don't you know, God responded to me through a Prophet who didn't know me? I was feeling a little shameful realizing that God heard that half of thought. The next thought that crossed my mind was what my co-workers must have thought of me praying a healing prayer, and then Barry died. God's response through this Prophet was, "know matter how much faith you have, and know matter how much you pray, nothing can change the appointed time." Then he said to me, Barry WAS healed. It took me a while to realize that Barry was healed when I saw him sitting on the cloud. As for the concern about what my co-workers thought, God's response through the prophet was "obedience." All he asked, is that I was obedient.

God will surely get his message across to us. We won't always understand why things happen the way they do. But we must **trust in the Lord with all thine heart; and lean not unto thine own understanding.**

In all thy ways acknowledge him, and he shall direct thy paths. (Proverbs 3:5-6 KJV) Some things we will understand better by and by. That's a song, but it rings true.

Two weeks later, my Aunt Lois, (my father's sister) died. She had cancer as well, and I was believing for her healing. When she died, emotionally, I lost it. I cried, "I'm sick of cancer killing people!" God quickly let me know, cancer didn't kill my aunt; it was her appointed time.

Well that revelation, along with the experience of Barry's memorial service motivated me to speak at my aunt's home going service. This wasn't a normal practice for our family, and it certainly was a first for me. But I never felt more confident about speaking. After all, I had something to say.

The service was out of town, three and a half hours away. My stomach was upset for days, but I went anyway. When I drove onto the church parking lot, I began experiencing shortness of breath. An overwhelming feeling of grief came over me like never before. It would overwhelm me for about a minute or so, and then disappear. These feelings of grief came repeatedly.

After confiding in my sister about how I was feeling, I regained my composure for minutes at a time. I asked my dad to walk in the church with me to view my aunt's body. Once inside the church, I immediately started trembling. My knees were buckling, and I was feeling out of control. My vision was blurred from the tears that filled my eyes. Still, I managed to see my aunt. I had never seen anyone so beautiful. She looked as if she were asleep. She looked so peaceful.

The drama continues. Still noticeably trembling and unable to get myself together, I constantly apologized to my dad. I didn't want my crying to upset him. I knew he was being strong for everyone else. My dad walked with me outside of the church. He handed me a piece of candy, in hopes that it would help me pull myself together. (Thank you daddy).

I went back to my sister, and shared with her that I had to continue to take deep breaths for fear of passing out. I told her I should have never said I would speak. I admitted to her that I couldn't do it. She looked at me strangely and said, "you better not pass out."

I began talking to God silently as fast as I could think.

"God I can't do this!"

"Who do I think I am?"

"I can't even stop crying!"

"I can't stop shaking!"

I kept taking deep breaths, as that was the only thing I knew to do. Finally, I calmed down. The pastor of the church came to me, and asked if I were the niece who wanted to speak. I reluctantly said yes. He told me to go sit in the pulpit. As I walked to the pulpit, I prayed.

"God please help me?"

"I can't do this without you!"

"I don't want to cry!"

"I don't want to stutter!"

"Please! Help me God."

I could see my family lining up at the door to come in the church. As they began walking in, most of them were crying. Suddenly, I had a burst of confidence, and with that, my demeanor began to change from total sobbing to strength. God raised me. I stood tall with dried tears. I watched them walk in as if they weren't even my family. It was like an out of body experience. I was amazed. I noticed my stomach had stopped hurting. Out of my mouth words were calmly flowing like, Bless God. I felt like a preacher standing there.

The pastor caught me off guard. He asked if I would say the prayer of comfort in the absence of one of the ministers. I said yes, and my mind went blank. I remember thanking God I didn't know ahead of time, or I would have been in distress. When I stood up, not having a clue what I would say, the words shot out of my mouth like a canon ball.

"I WILL bless the Lord at all times: his praise shall continually be in my mouth. My soul shall make her boast in the LORD: the humble shall here thereof, and be glad. O magnify the LORD with me, and let us exalt his name together. I sought the LORD, and he heard me, and delivered me from all my fears." (Psalm 34:1-4 KJV) ... my words followed, concluding the prayer.

After the prayer, I was given the okay to speak about my aunt. God had already given me encouraging words for my family. He strengthened me to say those words with a smile might I add. I will never forget how God stepped in and took over that day. Because of his intervention, I know in any given situation, I can call on Him and He will come to my rescue.

We prepared to go to the grave. Tears began to stream down my face. My vision was yet again blurred. I thought, Oh Lord! Here we go. The pastor quickly put me in the line of ministers and we proceeded to the site. I didn't have a clue what I was doing, but God knew. There the pastor nudged me, and said, "Go ahead, Pray." I had never done anything short of crying at a funeral service before, let alone pray.

Now do I have to tell you that truly, all of that was the glory of the Lord experienced and seen. Experienced by me, and seen of others who knew me. Only God could have given me such strength. Only the Holy Spirit could have brought back to my remembrance, things on the inside of me, in which I prayed. Only God kept me from falling flat on my face. I have nothing to boast of.

After the home going service, I understood that God wanted me to experience the impact of the grief some of my family members were going through. He wanted my words to be more than simply mere words. I have to admit, I was thankful, but I told God I didn't ever want to feel that type of grief again. It was no joke. It was almost unbearable.

Sometimes in our own pain, the glory of the Lord will manifest itself. I thank God that because of the death of my co-worker Barry and my aunt, and all He shared with me concerning them, I now have a new perspective on death. We need to stop labeling people's death with illnesses, murder and accidents. The bible didn't say we would all die to some disease or tragedy. It said we're all appointed a time to die, and no man knows the day or the hour.

• **Vacation**

Another time I saw the glory of the Lord was when I needed to get away. I was long overdue for a vacation. I kept telling my husband, "let's go somewhere." At that point, I didn't care if we walked across the street. I needed a break from it all.

I was believing God for restoration in a lot of areas. Physically, I was totally beat. My husband wasn't quite ready to take a vacation. It was different for him. He was retired.

I took my concerns to God. You know, the whole whining routine. God told me to pack. Well, I did just that, and I hid the suitcase. My husband wasn't one to plan long drawn out trips or vacations. He did things at the spur of the moment. From where I sat, I didn't see any evidence of us going anywhere anytime soon. But because I trusted God, I packed that suitcase with clothes for Florida.

About a week later, I got a phone call at work from my husband. He wanted to know if I would be ready to go to Disney World the next day. He also wanted to drive this time. Well all that said to me was, "Much Quality Time." See how it pays to be obedient. I didn't have to lift a finger planning, nor be concerned about any spending money. When God does it, He goes all out.

The three of us (our daughter included) drove to Disney World. I was excited. I had the music blasting. God ministered to me through the song, "Today is the first day of the best days of your life. The best is yet to come." You know the song. I was grinning from ear to ear, and receiving every word.

I looked up to the sky and saw what looked like a window carved in the clouds. The sun was shining brightly through the opening of the window. I heard God say, "See if I won't pour out a blessing that you won't have room enough to receive." I was so over-joyed, I was about to burst. God was truly pouring out the blessings. It was a vacation to remember. I felt special.

I've experienced God in so many other ways, through songs, people of course, and even in questioning another saints gift. Be careful who you make fun of. I remember I asked God for the gift of tongues. (For those of you who don't believe in tongues, that's fine, but keep reading, this is interesting). There's a moral to the story.

- **Mocking**

I wanted to speak in tongues for the sole purpose of using it when praying. I wanted the power folk talked about. I even visited another denomination with the belief that I would tarry in this little room with people standing over me until I began speaking in tongues. Well it didn't happen for me. (Here's a valuable lesson, when you're seeking something from God, go to God to get it).

I remember one day taking a long look at my life. I had more concerns than I could handle, and I didn't know what to do about any of them. I prayed and still I didn't know what to do. Out of desperation I told God, I would not touch another drop of food until He told me something. I was not going to eat until He talked to me. I began fasting and praying. I was determined, if God didn't talk to me, then I would die to starvation. I had never been more serious.

On the third evening of the fast, I was feeling a little weak. I was working late when one of my co-workers gave me a CD to listen to. I really didn't want to listen to this CD. I figured it just wasn't my type of music. But since her office was beside my work space, I played the CD. It was by Charlotte Church. This style of music was much different from the preferred gospel I was use to. However, I found it to be relaxing all the same.

Within minutes of listening to the CD, God spoke to me regarding the concerns I had. This was the first time I had ever heard God speak. Yet, I wasn't afraid. I was listening as if my very life depended on his every word. IT DID.

God responded to each of my concerns one by one, and there were many. After addressing all of my concerns but one, God told me to go to the bathroom and not claim the comp time for the period that I was in the bathroom. There, he addressed my final concern. He asked me why I wanted the gift of tongues. He talked to me about my motives for wanting the gift.

Once I assured God that I understood the purpose

of tongues, He told me to receive it. I received the gift the best I knew how, but from what I could see, nothing was happening. I mean, I didn't hear any strange words coming out of my mouth. I had my mouth wide open waiting. (Sounds silly, huh!)

Much time went by. I had forgotten about the gift of tongues. Then one day, I was watching T.V. and Benny Hinn came on. You know, the well-groomed man with the grayish white hair. He often wears a white suit. He comes on TBN (Trinity Broadcasting Network.) He has a healing ministry, "This is Your Day."

During the healing service, some of the things I saw him do simply didn't cut it for me. He called people to the stage, and as he lifted his hands, they fell to the floor. It really took the cake when he blew air on people and they fell to the floor. I was thinking that his breath was knocking people out. People were getting out of wheelchairs, claiming they could walk. People who couldn't hear were claiming to hear. People with diseases were claiming to be healed.

I began mocking Benny Hinn. I was convinced beyond a shatter of a doubt, this man was phony. I considered myself to be rather sane, and rational, but this man was going too far. I said, "Lord, I believe in you, but this man is fake." Immediately, I was stretched out on the living room floor, speaking in tongues. It was rather strange, and I couldn't believe those foreign words were coming out of my mouth. I got up off the floor totally amazed by what happened, but I dismissed it. I said again, "God he's still fake." Would you believe, that I was stretched out on the floor, speaking in tongues again? Finally, I said, "Okay God, I get it, he's not fake."

I always knew healing came from God. I now know that God also uses his anointing to flow through others, to bring forth healing. It's God's healing power working through people, allowing others to be healed. People can't heal people. God heals people. All that time I was asking for the gift of tongues and trying to receive it as God said, but it just hadn't come forward until I challenged one of God's children.

We can't do anything in our own strength, but we can do all things through Christ who strengthens us. Regardless to your upbringing, or what you're accustomed to, the key to remember is, all good gifts come from God. I learned from that mocking experience, just because you don't quite understand someone's gift, and because it might not sit well with you, or, because it looks abnormal to you, doesn't make it so. That experience helped to give me a greater appreciation for the gift of speaking in tongues and the gift of healing.

• Undying Love

Another time I saw the glory of the Lord concerning my husband. I use to question why I loved him so much. Don't misunderstand me, from day one, he was always a very sweet, considerate, and giving man. He showered me with gifts. He poured out compliments. He supported me in the things I wanted to do. He was romantic and sexy. He made me laugh. His smile warmed my heart. The man was handsome, and he made me weak at the knees. I can say all of that because he was/is my husband. He was my world. I felt safe with him. He was my night and shining armor. He was my Man.

It seemed no matter what he did or how he behaved, I automatically fell back into this love mode. I couldn't figure it out. I got to the point where it was even sickening to me. My mom once said, our entire family is like leeches. We grab on and won't let go. I didn't think that was good. But what I got from it was, we were prone to putting our total mind, body and soul into a relationship. We didn't hold back. Once we loved you, we loved you. We were committed.

I asked God, "Why do I love this man so much? Am I sick? What's wrong with me? Am I desperate? Am I obsessed? What is it?" He told me, He allowed me to see my husband the way He saw him. He gave me an unconditional love for him. Later, I came to the realization that it took the love of God for me to hang in there. Had I not seen my husband as the man God saw him as, I honestly don't think we would have survived.

I say love hurts, but I know God created us all, and He loves us all. I know God is love, and it doesn't hurt Him to love us. He doesn't have to put forth an effort to love us. However, loving us has nothing to do with hating the sin we commit. We can love a person and hate the wrongdoing of that person as well. But we're still commanded to love others as God loves. He said, love your neighbor as yourself. That's the second greatest commandment.

God sees us as fearfully and wonderfully made

and precious in his sight. We don't always see people as precious. Nor do we see them as wonderfully made. We're constantly looking on the outer man. God sees the inner man. He sees us as ambassadors with Himself and joint heirs with Jesus. He sees his child whom Jesus died for.

We, too, have to see the person as God sees him. In my own life, I was no saint, but I strived for holiness. Though I fell short every day, God still saw my potential. He saw what I would become, not what I was. We have to hold on to what God shows us about people. In doing so, you will see the glory of the Lord. In doing so, you will have what you're suppose to have anyway, agape love (unconditional love). When you do it God's way, you will go even deeper, having an undying love for the person. Now, that's love.

When I got the revelation of this undying love for my husband, of course Satan tried to throw a dagger in it. Here comes the monkey wrench. I spoke at a church down south for Mother's Day. I gave a testimony about this love for my husband. Practically everyone who knew me already knew of this love. After returning home, Satan said, "Oh you think you have unconditional love for your husband, huh. Well take this, and we'll see."

Without going into details, let me just say, Satan launched an attack against us. The situation before me was truly a blow to the pit of my stomach. I felt like I had been hit with a ton of bricks. You know Satan wants to try to make everything contrary to the Word of God. He wants you to think you're never going to see what God has promised. Sometimes he will even fill your mind with wrong ways to respond to the attack after he has launched it. Don't get side tracked; you know what's right and wrong behavior.

Of course I was angry at what appeared to have taken place. So angry, steam was probably coming out of my ears. I knew I had every right to be angry. I knew the bible said, be angry, but sin not. But the sin not part wasn't on my mind. I was so angry I felt like I had a nervous twitch. I thought I was going to blow a fuse. A part of me was in disbelief by what was happening. What happened? The bigger question is, How did I respond to what happened?

I was, indeed, surprised by my own actions. After the ordeal, instead of yelling, fussing, and saying what I could, or would have said, an increased utterance came forth. The only clear words I could utter were JESUS! JESUS! JESUS! I was hitting my leg out of anger and yelling JESUS! I fell to my knees, and nothing came out of my mouth but unknown language. It must have gone on for at least 45 minutes or longer.

The Holy Spirit was doing some serious interceding for me, and over the situation in prayer. I didn't know what to pray. In fact, if I had to think of a prayer, I'm sure it would not have been pleasing in God's sight. Now, I just want you to know that the mere fact that I didn't flick off was the glory of the Lord being demonstrated.

That kind of reaction can't be planned. My emotions were in overdrive, but God was doing the steering. I praise God for taking over my thoughts that day. That attack alone could have easily caused me to do a Rambo or turn into Sybil, with split personalities. I could have gone buck wild. I could have gone completely ballistic.

I said all that to say, some things we go through, we have no control over. On the other hand, some things we bring on ourselves. Beware of the saying, if you go looking for trouble, you will find it. There's truth to that statement. But I also know of a saying, "whatever is done in the dark will soon come to the light." I believe if you stay in sin long enough, God will openly reveal your sin to the world.

The point I'm trying to make is, you too, can love as God loves, and you're supposed to. That incident angered me tremendously, and it threw me for a loop. But it didn't change the love I had for my husband. So Satan was still defeated in his conquest of trying to sabotage the love I had for him. Don't allow the enemy to defeat you. Stop and see God's glory in your own life. It's there.

6

Receive Healing

Yes, there's a healing process. I remember thinking,

"Oh God! I'm going to die trying to deny my flesh!"

"This is hard! It hurts!"

"It seems like I don't have any control over my life. It's not fair!"

"I'm tired. I can't continue going through the same thing. I want it to end."

"How Long God?"

"Why me God?"

"I don't have to take this!"

" Maybe I'll just stop caring."

Before I could take on the attitude of not caring anymore, I was lead to read **(Psalm 147:3 NIV)** which says, **He heals the brokenhearted and binds up their wounds.**

You know it's easy to walk away from a problem,

and it's easy to give up. But my question is, "Will you take God at his word?" When the going gets rough, "Will you quit?" I was broken hearted, and I had many open wounds. But one day it dawned on me, those wounds would remain open and even become infected if they didn't receive the proper attention. I realized I needed to seek healing. I realized I needed help to stay the course.

Will you bail out? Or will you say, "God, I'm in this for the long haul." I know you've heard of long suffering, and it means just what it says, to suffer L O N G. It means enduring through the suffering with patience and hope.

If you profess to be a Christian (one who has accepted Jesus as Lord and Savior), a disciple (a follower of Christ), **(Hebrews 12:1-3 NAS)** tells us, **THEREFORE, SINCE we have so great a cloud of witnesses surrounding us, let us also lay aside every encumbrance,** (every weight, every thing that hinders us) **and the sin which so easily entangles us, and let us run with endurance** (patience, perseverance) **the race that is set before us, fixing our eyes on Jesus, the author and perfecter of faith, who for the joy set before Him endured the cross, despising the shame, and has sat down at the right hand of the throne of God. For consider Him who has endured such hostility by sinners against Himself, so that you may not grow weary and lose heart.**

Somebody's always watching. Everybody has an opinion. Nobody has all the answers. Just remember, there is nothing you will ever encounter that God doesn't understand. He knows your pain. He hears your cry, and He will deliver you from the hands of the enemy. He will deliver you from evil and wickedness. Know that there is no situation in life that you could ever encounter that is worse than the gruesome death of Jesus.

Don't lose heart. We're all faced with daily tests, and we can pass them. **Do you not know that those who run in a race all run, but only one receives the prize? Run in such a way that you may win. (1 Corinthians 9:24 NAS)** You can't win a race running with a defeated attitude. You can't run as if your legs were filled with lead. How can you win if you're barely lifting your feet off the ground? You have to get moving, put some pep in your step.

In this spiritual race, as we allow God to take residence in our mind and body, healing will come. We have to stop closing our spirit to God's truth. Jesus is our bread of life, and He wants to feed us. If you believe Jesus is the bread of life, eat from Him and hunger no more. Be healed.

I got to the point where I wanted to receive healing badly. I was tired of feeling the way I felt. I just wanted God to control me. I knew if He did, I wouldn't struggle so much. I was aware that we would have problems, but I knew God could handle them all. I figured the more in tune I was with His word, the easier it would be for me going through. Trust me, it's easier going through anything with God than without God. I tried it both ways.

Because of the state I was in, I was driven to take a long, hard look at my marriage. The thought that continuously went through my mind was after all my years of sacrificing, I wasn't going to allow anyone or any thing to prevent me from reaping my benefits. Nothing was going to stand in the way of what I spent so much of my life working toward, waiting for, and believing in. I knew I had to receive healing in order to begin to reap my harvest.

Healing comes in many dimensions, and I needed it every way possible. We need to receive healing emotionally, spiritually, physically and mentally. I received healing of the mind, body and soul.

- **Healing of the Mind**

My mind worked overtime. I entertained negative thoughts. I visualized negative things. I even responded out loud to some of my thoughts. I asked a question and answered it. I allowed my thoughts to determine my mood. My thoughts often were at the center of my frustration.

Some of the things that consumed my mind were very real, but I found, if you allow your mind to play tricks on you, it will deceive you. Eventually, you'll see things that aren't there. You will hear things that weren't said. You will imagine things that didn't occur. It's a dangerous state of mind to be in.

This state of mind wants to keep you suspicious, jealous, envious, paranoid and filled with distrust. I'm paraphrasing Isaiah 26:3, if you keep your mind focused on the things of God, He will keep your heart in perfect peace. But continue to allow your mind to wallow in confusion, discord, and strife, and you will soon be facing insanity. You don't want to go there.

We have to unclutter our minds. Be careful what you listen to. Be careful what you look at, and be careful of the company you keep. If only junk goes in, then only junk will come out. Fill your mind with positive, healthy things. If you're reading something that adds onto your negative thoughts, stop reading it. If you're watching things that tempt you to do wrong, don't watch them. If you're going places that feast on negativity, don't go there. If you're around negative people who are always giving you negative advice or always bashing people, stay away from them. Protect your mind. We've heard it said before, but truly, "A Mind is a Terrible Thing to Waste." Reclaim your mind Today.

- **Healing of the Body**

God freed my body from illness, not only to testify of his goodness, but so that I could also concentrate more on the things He wanted to accomplish through me. How can we offer our total service to God if we're walking time bombs?

I was having shortness of breath. I had rapid heartbeats. The pulsation left me feeling like I was having panic or anxiety attacks. I was awakened in the middle of the night to these attacks and in hot sweats. Heat triggered the attacks. Hot baths triggered them. Caffeine triggered them. Sometimes, just sitting still in a relaxed position triggered them. The palpitations would last anywhere from 20 to 45 minutes. After each episode, I was drained.

The final episode that scared me into realizing I needed to go to the hospital was while having palpitations, when I tried to talk, I struggled with the use of my words. I could only stutter. I knew at that moment, I had to face reality and get some help.

Would you believe with all these afflictions, although I had been to the doctor on numerous occasions, I still had not asked God for healing? My attitude was I'm not going anywhere until I get my promises. I was certain, I wouldn't die until God fulfilled his promises concerning my life regardless to the ailments I had.

One morning around 6:00 a.m. I was preparing to go out of town for my uncle's funeral. I was told he suffered a heart attack and died. That morning I was experiencing shortness of breath, but I was determined to make the three and a half hour trip. Besides, my God-mother/Aunt was looking forward to seeing me.

The T.V. was on. Creflo Dollar was preaching. The man literally jumped out of the T.V. and touched me on the shoulder and said, "Look, if you don't stop, you will die before you get your promise." He said some other things that hit hard, too. I panicked. I called my mother and told her I wouldn't make the home going service. I told my husband I wasn't feeling well. We jumped in the car and went to the emergency room.

The doctors did an EKG, and other tests. I was diagnosed with a heart disease called Mitral Valve Prolapse, (a heart disease that couldn't be cured). They said it had nothing to do with diet or exercise. I immediately thought, "These people are crazy. They don't know what they're talking about." Moments later, I was informed that I had a cyst on my lung. I thought to myself, "How in the world do you get a cyst on your lung?" In addition to that diagnosis, I was previously diagnosed with a heart condition called PSVT (Parasysmal Super Ventricular Track), a heart condition that's often misdiagnosed because of symptoms of panic and anxiety attacks. I was also diagnosed with a heart murmur and an irregular heartbeat.

Well, I was getting impatient with the doctors. I was tired of laying there, and I was hungry. I didn't want to hear what they were saying. I unhooked the wires, got dressed, and told the nurse to tell the doctor I was leaving. I had been there too long. Now, was that stupid or what? Warning, don't try that. Immature Alert! It's one thing to have faith, but be sure you're exercising faith and not ignorance.

When I went back to work, I told my supervisor what the doctor said. She searched the internet. She wanted to see what all that meant. She came back and told me what she found. She almost scared the life out of me. I didn't realize the seriousness of my health. I called the doctor back and scheduled follow up appointments.

As time went on, I felt bad most of the time. I was young, but had more concerns than the average elderly person. I was in bad shape. Walking from work to the parking lot where I parked daily was strenuous exercise for me. I was out of breath by the time I got to my car. My heart raced anytime it chose to. I always felt like someone had just frightened me, or chased me.

A lady name Liz, invited me to go with her and a friend to a Healing Crusade in Pennsylvania. She didn't know I had all these illnesses. She asked me to go for company purposes. Guess who was holding the crusade, Benny Hinn. (Ha Ha Ha)

I got there, and oh my goodness, the anointing in that place was unexplainable. People were being healed. The anointing was causing people to fall down (but not get hurt). People were praising and worshiping God. I was shouting and didn't care who heard me. I was crying hysterically. I felt good, but weird at the same time. I knew what I was doing, but I didn't want to stop. I was reaching and grabbing in the air. I guess I was trying to grab God (smile). I was jumping, but I wasn't out of place. Everywhere I looked, others were doing the same or more. After seeing all those people, I even understood my worship better.

Finally, Benny Hinn said, "The anointing is here." It was obvious that the presence of the Lord was there. Benny Hinn said, "Put your hand on your illness." I put my hand on my heart, and immediately felt this tremendous heat all over me. I had never felt that before. The only heat I was familiar with was the heat I felt on my bottom when my mom was getting ready to spank me as a form of discipline.

This heat/warmth had such an impact that I knew it was God healing me. I knew without a doubt that I was healed right there on the spot. I immediately thanked God for healing me. Since God is so gracious, and in him there is no lack, I also received healing for my daughter, who had similar symptoms.

She wasn't at the crusade, but that's not a stipulation with God. This was all based on faith.

God miraculously healed me of all those illnesses simontaneously in that healing service. I never made it to the stage as they air on T.V. No human laid hands on me. The presence of God was there. Healing was available, and I gladly received it.

Later, I went back to the doctor. I told the heart specialist that God healed me. He disregarded what I said as if I weren't even speaking. He didn't even address it. His only response was that I still needed to take the medicine, just in case. I left his office talking aloud to myself, "I know God healed me."

Listen, I know God gave us doctors. I know sometimes we need to take advantage of their skills and services, and sometimes medication is necessary. But when God overrides the doctor's diagnosis, we need to joyfully accept it. He is the great Physician.

That same day, I went to the second doctor who had x-rayed my lungs. He said, "Yes, you definitely had a cyst on your lung, but it's gone now." I told him that God had healed me. He said he believed it, and he thanked me for coming back to share that with him.

After being healed, I was able to do things I hadn't been able to do. I participated in the Race for the Cure of Breast Cancer. People who knew of my illness but didn't quite believe in my healing advised me not to walk in the race. Not only did I walk, I ran as well. I finished in great time. I no longer had palpitations, shortness of breath, anxiety or panic attacks, flutters, hot sweats or any of the previous symptoms. Praise God! My body felt good. I was truly a new person. I was also a grateful person and a witness to how God miraculously heals.

The other side of receiving healing is not allowing Satan or anyone else to tell you that you weren't healed. About a week or so after my healing, as I got in the bathtub; the symptoms I experienced before my healing appeared to come back. Immediately, I prayed. I stood on my healing. After all, healed meant healed.

After professing total healing, the symptoms never came back again. Satan doesn't want us to believe we received healing. He wants to fool you into thinking the symptoms are still there, and you were never really healed. Don't believe the lie. Hold on to your healing.

God even healed me of terrible migraines. I had migraines so bad, I could barely see. When the migraines came, I missed weeks at a time from work. I could barely function. The lights bothered me, as well as sound, and movement. The pain was sharp, throbbing, and lasted for days. Every time I turned around, I had a headache.

The pain was almost like a stabbing effect in the center of my left eye. Sometimes, the pain would shift to the center of my head, and it would be dull and nagging. But always, whether dull or nagging, the pain was persistent. Only applied pressure would minimize the pain. Whew! I tried ice. I tried heat. I took 800 milligrams of Motrin like candy.

You know the commercial, I have a headache and it's screaming Excedrin. Well Excedrin didn't help me, and my head hurt so bad I couldn't scream anything. I tried every pill the doctors could think of. I was feeling like a Ginny pig. I even wondered if the doctors were giving me placebos. Thank God for healing.

It's not God's will that any of us remain in sickness or bondage. God doesn't cause sickness, but He sometimes allows situations. We have to trust God with our bodies as well as our minds. When He gives us warning signs, we need to take heed. Example: If caffeine triggers your illness, cut it back, or cut it out. Sure you'll go through withdrawal, but the end result is worth it. Caffeine was bad for my heart, but when I didn't drink it in the form of sodas, I got headaches. I had such an addiction that I lusted, and was in agony when I stopped drinking sodas. But by the grace of God, and many years after my healing, I denied my flesh of sodas of any kind. They were causing more harm than good.

• **Healing of the Soul**

God healed my soul when he showed me that, just believing in him was not enough. **If you use your mouth to say, "Jesus is Lord," and if you believe in your heart that God raised Jesus from death, then you will be saved. We believe with our hearts, and so we are made right with God. And we use our mouths to say that we believe, and so we are saved. As the Scripture says, "Anyone who trusts in him will never be disappointed." That Scripture says "anyone" because there is no difference between Jew and non-Jew. The same**

Lord is the Lord of all and gives many blessings to all who trust in him. The Scripture says, "Anyone who asks the Lord for help will be saved."(Romans 10:9-13 NCV)

My soul was wandering, searching, and not satisfied. When you're made in God's image, naturally you're going to feel a longing for him. It may take some longer to figure out who they're longing for. But eventually it is revealed to you, and the choice will be yours to make, as to whether or not you accept the one in whom image you were made.

I was active in two churches growing up, but I didn't grow up with this complete teaching about salvation. I was taught if I believed in God, I would go to heaven. Somewhere along the line, emphasis on confessing and believing was lost. I now know there's a two-part process. We have to confess with our mouth that Jesus is Lord, and believe in our hearts that God raised Jesus from the dead. It's quite simple. I don't understand why people leave any part of this truth out.

I also had to realize that I was born with a sinful nature. I was an enemy of God. Jesus came to earth so that I would have life, and life more abundantly. He died as the ultimate sacrifice for my sins. He died for the remission of my sins. He was without sin. He was the only sacrifice that was acceptable to take away the sins of the World by the shedding of his blood. He paid a penalty I owed but couldn't pay. He took on my punishment, giving me the right to eternal life.

Because of this ultimate sacrifice, not only do we have eternal life, but sin no longer has authority over us. We're no longer bound to sin. We have a choice to sin, or not to sin. Thank God. He always has a ram in the bush. He used that ram to make the good news of the gospel available to me, and as a result, I received eternal life.

Now instead of damnation, my spirit eternally resides with God. My heart's desire is that every person who reads these words is able to say, and know for certain, he has eternal life (ever lasting life, with Jesus Christ). It all boils down to using your mouth to confess and your heart to believe.

Don't you want healing for your Soul?

7

Surrender

❦

"Okay God, I want to move forward but I need you to show me how."

Aren't you tired of repeating the same cycles? I know I was. I could see the cycles coming, but I couldn't do anything about them because I hadn't surrendered to God.

What's keeping you from surrendering? Is it your relationship?

Could it be that your mate is a night owl?

Does your mate take long trips and exclude you?

Is he or she suddenly secretive with cell phones/pagers/emails?

Are the two of you falsely accusing each other of things?

Has the communication shut down?

Is the intimacy lacking? Do you feel neglected?

Are you feeling you're always giving and seldom on the receiving end?

Are you feeling overwhelmed?

Are you having problems reaching out?

Do you feel disrespected? How about unappreciated? Have you been lied to?

Do you feel you're being used as a doormat?

Are you taking mental or emotional abuse?

Are you struggling to trust again? Are you desiring to be trusted again?

Well, I feel ya! You want to surrender, but you get caught up in feeling that you'll be giving in to the situation or the circumstance. You may be feeling like you're giving in to defeat, when in actuality, you're giving in to God. You may be feeling a sense of helplessness, but God says, "give it to Him and He will help you get through." If you want to help the process along, surrender. Let go, and let God. Stop interfering. His grace is sufficient for you.

When faced with continued challenges in my relationship, I'll tell you what I said.

"God I surrender!"

"Help me to Deny my Self!"

"Do what you will with me, and my life."

Like Tina Turner said, "But baby don't you know, that I don't wanna hurt no more."

"Don't care now who's to blame, I don't really wanna fight no more."

Sometimes you just don't care who's wrong or right, you just don't want to hurt no more.

"God I've done everything in my power, and nothing seems to works. Tell me what to do?"

"God help me, Please!"

I cried buckets of tears, until my eyes were blood shot. But my tears weren't enough. They didn't move God, and they sure didn't move Satan. My words weren't even enough. Then finally, **(Ephesians 6:13-18 KJV)** stood out, **Wherefore take unto you the whole armour of God, that ye may be able to withstand in the evil day, and having done all, to stand. Stand therefore, having your loins girt about with truth, and having on the breastplate of righteousness; and your feet shod with the preparation of the gospel of peace. Above all, taking the shield of faith, wherewith ye shall be able to quench all the fiery darts of the wicked. And take the helmet of salvation, and the sword of the Spirit, which is the word of God. Praying always with all prayer and supplication in the Spirit, and watching thereunto with all perseverance and supplication for all saints.**

If you take this scripture to heart, you will find it easier to surrender. Donnie McKlurkin said, "After you've done all you can, you just stand," and where did that come from?

(Ephesians 6:13-18) How long will you continue to be robbed of your peace? Choose your battles. It's not necessary to try to fight them all, nor is it necessary to try to fight them alone. By doing so, you are simply setting yourself up for failure. Don't allow yourself to become physically, mentally, emotionally or spiritually depleted. Life challenges sometimes have a way of emptying us.

As we surrender, God honors our yielded spirit. The scripture says that **God will turn our wailing**

into dancing. He will remove our sackcloth and clothe us with joy. He will gird us with gladness, that our heart may sing to him and not be silent. Feast on God and His goodness. He promises to take care of you. He will show you how to surrender unto Him in every area. If you take that first step toward Him, He will strengthen you to do the rest. Allow his perfect will to be done in your life as it is written in Heaven.

8

Tactics of the Enemy

❧

S atan heard you surrender to God. Although he can't stop you from surrendering, he goes into his bag of tricks, and pulls out the Tactics of the Enemy Card. See he doesn't want you to walk in the marvelous light. He wants to keep you in darkness. He doesn't care about your past, present or future hurt, pain, disappointment or sickness. He doesn't care how long you've been a wreck. He wants to wreck your life even more. **Be careful! Watch out for attacks from the Devil, your great enemy. He prowls around like a roaring lion, looking for some victim to devour. (1 Peter 5:8 NLT)**

The thing we must never forget is Satan is very real. Remember Lucifer? He was an angel adorned with lights. He decided he wanted to be like God. He was thrown from heaven. He became Satan, the serpent, the enemy, the deceiver, the father of lies. We should not under estimate his power. But at the same token, know that Satan is a defeated foe. Of course, we are no-match for him alone. But that's okay; God is our advocate. He is our shield, and He protects us from Satan. He fights our battles. Satan is no match for God.

- **Tactic #1 Drugs/Alcohol**

I was 18 years old. I lived down south, where we called it "The Country." I attended my cousin's wedding reception. They served alcoholic beverages. As discretely as I could, I had several mixed drinks. Let's just say I drank heavily that evening without my parents knowing or seeing me. Not only was I drinking, but unfortunately for me, a young lady was in the area from Washington, D.C. who was known for carrying and using drugs. I'll admit, occasionally I smoked marijuana, but I always made it clear, that was the furthest I would go when it came to using drugs.

I was outside in a parked car with this young lady smoking marijuana when it hit me, she had given me something different. She then told me it was boat (marijuana laced with embalming fluid). I was upset with her and immediately went back inside. Within seconds, I began hallucinating beyond my wildest imagination.

The lights appeared to be flashing. As I danced, I felt like I was constantly blinking back and forth between two dance floors. When I looked up, it appeared I was dancing fast as if I was on dance fever or soul train. When I looked down, it appeared I was dancing slow and in a provocative way. To this day, I don't know what type of dance I was actually doing once I began hallucinating.

The steps appeared to be moving toward me. Women whom I didn't know appeared to be looking at me in a lustful way. I remember feeling very scared and panicky. Not knowing what to do, I felt the only person who could help me was another cousin, a mutual friend of the person who gave me the drugs. I tried to get her attention, but she couldn't see the seriousness of the situation at the time. She was having fun and wanted to continue dancing.

I knew I was on my own and I had to do something fast. I didn't want my parents to find out. I went to the bathroom and hid there until someone knocked on the door. I could see the light shining through the bathroom window. I felt like it was drawing me. I felt a sense of security from the light. I stayed there as long as I could. Eventually, I had to leave my only place of security. There was only one restroom for women, and people needed to use it.

After the reception, I made it home without causing any attention to myself. For the next two weeks or so, I stared into space. I was not my usual self. Mom asked what was wrong with me; of course I didn't tell her. I played it off the best I could. I had to fight this one secretly.

The truth of the matter is I think the embalming fluid, however much I inhaled, killed some of my brain cells. People laugh when I say that, but after all, it is used to assure you're dead. It causes bodily functions to cease to function. I mention my brain cells because I was very good at spelling, even Spelling

Bee material, until the incident. Afterwards, my memory wasn't quite in tact. I couldn't remember as sharply as before. I even felt different.

You know the bible tells us to **Train up a child in the way he should go: and when he is old, he will not depart from it. (Proverbs 22:6 KJV)** Well, although I witnessed family members smoking and drinking, I wasn't trained to smoke and drink. I chose to do that. My parents taught me right from wrong. I thank them for the training and for my upbringing. Because of my training, even though I took it upon myself to do wrong, I still had the sense to pray my way through.

I remember praying as earnestly as I could. I told God if he helped me get through this, I would never touch another cigarette, drug or alcohol as long as I lived. God set me free from that snare, that tactic of the enemy in 1985. I have never turned back to alcohol or drugs of any sort. I don't even want any rum cake or candy with liquor. That's just how horrifying and life changing my experience was. I'm grateful to God for his mercy. I owe it to him to be obedient. I don't hold the young lady who gave me the drugs responsible for what I inhaled. We all make mistakes. Some mistakes are more costly than others. I never saw her again. I was told she's drug-free now. Praise God.

I never liked the taste of alcohol. Basically, I drank because after finally giving in to temptation, it was the in thing to do. I didn't have to purchase it. I didn't like to smoke because I was afraid to inhale the smoke. Free packages of cigarettes were made available to me. I didn't like marijuana. It made my breath stink. I knew 99% of my high was fake. I only indulged because I could use it as an excuse to act out of character. It was handed to me by the bag. The joints were already rolled for me. Now, of course I later learned that none of that stuff was free. It costs me in more ways than I expected. Anything that alters your personality comes with a price.

Now to show you how Satan tried to trap me. In 2000-2001, I was watching a television documentary where a man was telling how he got strung out on drugs. He said there's a feeling you get the first time you do drugs, and you search repeatedly to get that same feeling again. You never get that feeling again, and that's how you get hooked.

As that man talked, Satan said to me, "Yeah, but you're saved, and you're stronger now. You could use drugs and nothing would happen to you." I immediately said out loud, "That's the most stupid thing you could have ever said to me." See he's subtle. But what he didn't count on was my response, I had already made up my mind to die to alcohol and drugs more than 15 years ago.

Now doesn't that sound a lot like when Satan tried to tempt Jesus? **THEN JESUS was led by the Spirit into the desert to be tempted by the devil. After fasting forty days and forty nights, he was hungry. The tempter came to him and said, "If you are the Son of God, tell these stones to become bread." Jesus answered, "It is written: 'Man does not live on bread alone, but on every word that comes from the mouth of God."(Matthew 4:1-4 NIV)**

How are you going to tempt the one who is the bread of life, with bread? Of course Jesus couldn't be tempted, but that's a prime example of how Satan just keeps coming. **Then the devil took him to the holy city and had him stand on the highest point of the temple. "If you are the Son of God, he said, "throw yourself down. For it is written: He will command his angels concerning you, and they will lift you up in their hands, so that you will not strike your foot against a stone." Jesus answered him, "It is also written: Do not put the Lord your God to the test."(Matthew 4:5-7 NIV)**

That still wasn't good enough for Satan, he still had to give Jesus his best shot. He had to try one last time to tempt him. **Again the devil took him to a very high mountain and showed him all the kingdoms of the world and their splendor. "All this I will give you," he said, "if you will bow down and worship me." Jesus said to him, "Away from me, Satan! For it is written: 'Worship the Lord your God, and serve him only.' Then the devil left him, and angels came and attended him. (Matthew 4:8-11 NIV)**

Jesus knew who his father was. He knew that all he ever needed, his father had and would provide. Temptations will come, but just like Jesus, we, too, must recognize and resist the devil and he will surely flee.

- **Tactic #2 Adultery/Fornication**

Satan is patient. He will wait for you however long it takes, as long as he gets the results of entrapment. His subtlety and cunning spirit can cause you to fall prey to temptation if you're not watchful. That's why it's so easy for some to commit adultery or to fornicate.

Satan convinces you that you're lonely, and you're being deprived. If you're having problems in your relationship, Satan wants to convince you that you can have your needs met elsewhere. He works to plant thoughts of justification for wrongdoing in your mind. He wants you to think that if your mate commits adultery (sex outside of marriage) or fornication (sex before marriage), you should repay your mate by doing the same thing. He convinces you that by doing so, you'll feel whole again and satisfied. He wants you to believe that this act can and will fill the voids that you have.

Flee from sexual immorality. All other sins a man commits are outside of his body, but he who sins sexually sins against his own body. Do you not know that your body is a temple of the Holy Spirit, who is in you, whom you have received from God? You are not your own; you were bought at a price. Therefore honor God with your body. (1 Corinthians 6:18-20 NIV)

Sexual sin always hurts someone. It hurts God because it shows that we prefer following our own desires instead of the leading of the Holy Spirit. It hurts others because it violates the commitment so necessary to a relationship. Sooner or later you will experience the harmful effect: be it a failed relationship; separation or divorce; sexually transmitted diseases; unwanted pregnancies; abortions; division; bad reputations; guilt; or the mere fact that you sinned against God.

Adultery and fornication usually stem from looking for love in all the wrong places. You end up with lust and you're deceived into believing that it's love. Go to the One who is love and pour out your heart. Only God can truly satisfy you. Only God can demonstrate his perfect love through the one he has set aside for you.

So yes, it's a must that we die to fornication and adultery too. Denying your flesh in this area is very doable. If you're married, make your spouse the sole person you give your body to. The bed is undefiled in marriage only. Your body is his, and his body is yours. You're supposed to satisfy each other.

If you're single, abstain from sex for at least six months. Give your body time for cleansing and purification. It won't kill you to abstain from sex. Try it. You're not supposed to be having sex anyway. This sin is called fornication. If you continue in this act of sin, you will never receive the blessings God has for you.

Whether you're an adulterer or fornicator, you are held accountable for how you use your body. Maybe, you're cunning enough to hide it from your mate, but you can't hide from God. No good things will come from your lustful deed. Stop thinking that God doesn't care about you having improper sex. His word already told you how he felt about it.

- **Tactic #3 Materialism**

You can have what you consider to be the American Dream, and maybe even feel you've succeeded in life. But if you make idols your god, and material wealth is what keep you going, you'll soon be in for a rude awakening. What happens when you lose the wealth? You're left feeling devastated, humiliated, embarrassed, and materialistically you hit rock bottom. What you considered to be a safe haven is no longer there. Your false security is gone.

What good is it for a man to gain the world, and yet lose or forfeit his very self? (Luke 9:25 NIV) If you are lusting over material things, if acquiring stuff is more important to you than the one who created you, you need to do some serious soul searching. Decide to die to the lust of your eye. The more you see, the more you want, at any cost.

You have to choose this day whom you will serve. Will you serve God or things? Material things are temporal. They will only quench your thirst momentarily. It's a temporary cover up. Earthly security is uncertain, but God is always faithful. I know first hand, the hurt associated with material loss. I had what I thought was the American Dream. I had the big house, and everything in it was paid for. I didn't have the white picket fence, but I had the dog. Dixie was her name. She was Chow mixed with German Shepard. She resided in the garage.

There were two vehicles, one even luxurious. I had the husband whom I adored, and the child I so desperately desired. I had a good job. I even had decent clothes. But yet, I found myself sitting on the floor feeling sad and not able to explain my feelings. There was a deep void, and no matter how much stuff I got, I just wasn't fulfilled. I kept asking, What is it? Why am I feeling this emptiness? Often a sadness came upon me causing me to want to cry, and I couldn't explain why.

Over time, God showed me it was He that I was lacking. Yeah, sure I grew up in church. We went to Sunday School. I sang on the choir. I had been christened as a Lutheran. I had even been baptized as a Baptist. I had accepted Jesus as my Lord and Savior, but all that meant to me was when I died, I would go to heaven.

I went from practically every denomination to non denomination trying to find something to grasp onto. I knew the ten commandments. I knew the Lord's Prayer. I said my grace. I kneeled at bedtime to pray before going to sleep, sometimes. I knew the basics, but I didn't know enough to have a relationship with God. I knew of Him, but I didn't know Him.

Although all the material stuff I acquired was good to have, it didn't mean anything to me on the inside. Eventually, I lost the house and a vehicle. Dixie was gone. My credit was seared. The marriage was on the rocks. The clothes began to shrink. I no longer liked my job. I had fallen hard. But through it all, I gained something money couldn't buy. I gained something far greater than material wealth. I gained an intimate relationship with God. I had something more precious than gold, more precious than possessions.

So I moved from Hollywood to the Hood (my

inside joke), but my void had been filled. (It doesn't matter where you live, what matters is Who lives in you). That void which allowed emptiness and sadness to come in was filled with God's love, his goodness, kindness, his mercy and his grace. Although I had received salvation many years earlier, I never knew of God's peace (The peace that surpassed all understanding). I never knew of His joy (Unspeakable joy). I never knew how much He loved me. I never knew who I was in Him, and I never knew what I meant to Him.

I believe the more hardship I experienced, the greater my relationship with God grew. I learned, we should never allow anything, not people, wealth, education, careers, or our desires come before God. God wants our heart. He wants our all. He wants our yielded bodies and soul.

Delight yourself in the Lord and he will give you the desires of your heart. (Psalm 37:4 NIV) No good thing will the Lord withhold from you if you walk upright before Him. The things of God will last, and they will remain. What God gives, the world won't be able to take away from you.

The bottom line is, I now have more than I lost, and the best is yet to come. The bible also says, To whom much is given, much is required. Are you meeting the requirements? I wasn't.

9

Stages of Defeat

꿈꿈꿈

You see the tactics of the enemy, but yet you still fall into the stages of loneliness, depression, and maybe even attempted suicide. Sometimes, our version of love can be a funny thing. I'm sure we've all fallen in love at some point or another. We've grabbed onto Mr. or Miss. Right and held on for dear life.

I was a country girl, born in the city. I was naive to a lot of things. I gave folks the benefit of the doubt. When I opened up my heart to someone, it was wide open. I automatically assumed the person was trustworthy and had my best interest. It took me a while to realize, just because you're in love doesn't mean your world should only consist of you and that person.

It's never healthy to allow your entire life to evolve around any one person. One risk you take in doing so is being by yourself, feeling lonely, and secluded when things go wrong between you and that person. Allowing yourself to be put in such a position, subjects you to the lies of Satan. Satan wants you feeling down and out. He wants you to feel neglected and unloved; that way he can lead you astray. Never let him get you alone. He'll smooth talk you right on into depression.

- **Stage #1 Loneliness**

I remember years ago, sitting on the floor crying out to God because I was so lonely. I just wanted a hug. I wanted to feel wanted. I needed encouragement, but I wanted it from my husband. Then, I got this picture of Jesus when he was in the Garden of Gethsemane praying. He asked the disciples to watch for an hour while he prayed, and he came back twice only to find them asleep. He said to them, "could you not stay awake for one hour?" He was preparing for crucifixion, and here they were sleeping.

Although I thought what I was experiencing at that moment was crushing; when God showed me Jesus, first I thought about how Jesus must have felt in that garden. He couldn't count on the disciples at such crucial time. Second, I was encouraged to know that Jesus knew how I felt and what I was dealing with. I was able to see that the things I experienced didn't even compare to the suffering of Jesus. My prayer life couldn't even compare to Jesus'. I've never prayed so intensely that I sweat drops of blood.

Looking back, sometimes we are very selfish people. All we care about is our own agenda. When are we ever going to get pass ME ME ME ME ME?

"I hurt more than you. I've been through more than you." It's time to grow up. You know the saying, get off the bottle and onto the meat. It's time to grow into the things of the Lord.

The bigger picture is this, oftentimes the very thing we want from others, God says, get it from Him first. You know, **But seek ye first the Kingdom of God, and his righteousness; and all these things shall be added unto you. (Matthew 6:33 KJV)**

Now, back to the hug thing. God will always address your concerns. I asked God, "How can you hug me?" Don't ever underestimate the power of God. I was laying on the sofa one day and I asked God to hug me. Within seconds, I felt this warmth all around me. I felt his arms around me. It was truly a hug. It was soothing and so relaxing. I just wanted to stay there and bask in his love. I laid back into his arms and thanked him. Oh, it felt so good. No one can love you like Jesus can. No one can hold you like Jesus can. But if you're like me, I know you're saying, well, can my mate try anyway. (smile)

You know God demonstrated His love to us when He gave His only begotten son Jesus to die on the cross for us. That should have been enough. But He still continues to demonstrate His love to us and through us daily. As far as me feeling unwanted, God told me He wanted me. He told me how He took his time and made me. He said, **"See, I have engraved you on the palms of my hands; your walls are ever before me."(Isaiah 49:16 NIV)** Now it doesn't get any better than that. That should do something to your self-esteem. Unlike people, God is always available, and sometimes it needs to be just you and God, alone – not lonely. He will pamper you unlike any spa.

- **Stage #2 Depression/Suicide**

From loneliness to depression. That's where Satan wants you. He wants you to isolate yourself. He wants you to feel helpless. He wants to converse with you, sort of hang out with you in the spirit. How many of you know that's dangerous? You're too vulnerable. Meanwhile, Satan wants you to think he's your friend. He tells you that you have every right to feel what you feel, and act the way you act. NOT! Don't listen to him. His lies are straight from the pit of hell.

So you bypass loneliness and move into the depressed zone. This level gets more intense. Your emotions began to take a toll on you physically. You began experiencing an almost crushing feeling where you have to constantly take deep breaths. But that's still not deep enough in the pit; he wants you even deeper. You're crying often. At first, you hide the tears, you try to save them for private use. You find yourself praying for rain because at least when it's raining, if you're driving, people can't decipher between the rain and your tears.

Tears don't move Satan. He'll use that moment to plant thoughts of suicide in your mind. He told me one time, "you know, if you commit suicide, you will still go to heaven, because you're saved." Notice how Satan is always trying to use my salvation to tempt me. He must not know, although I entertain some of his thoughts or ideas, I'm secure in my salvation.

Meanwhile, you're talking to God and you're listening to Satan at the same time. Your anger increases. You're bitter. You feel you're at your wit's end. You begin telling yourself, nothing really matters. As you listen to the lies of Satan, they sound daring. Without your complete awareness, your outlook on life changes. All you really care about is you, and your feelings. You don't care about family. You're not considering how they would handle your loss should you give in; you really don't care at this moment.

In the midst of hearing God and Satan, a voice says, "If you commit suicide, people will say, I thought she was strong." "I thought she had faith." "I thought she was a Christian." "They'll see you as weak, and they'll talk about you." At this point of hearing the good versus the bad, you're not sure who is doing the talking. I knew what I couldn't get away with, but I wasn't sure what I could get away with.

I told Satan, "Look, I'm going to talk to you, but I'm not going to do anything crazy you tell me to do." Then I said, "Okay God, if I can't do anything to myself, and I can't do anything about the situation or to an actual person, and I can't leave the situation, then I'll just lay here in bed and die. I won't be bothered with anyone. I'll just sleep myself away." Bad mistake!

Soon, I began to feel as if the bed was pulling me deeper and deeper into the mattress. My voice began to fade. My arms and legs hurt and were weak. I started smelling vomit. Now that's disgusting. I kept asking myself, "Is that me? Pew! That stinks." I tried to jump up, and go to the bathroom, only to find I could barely walk. I didn't realize with all the stress and pressure associated with depression how frail my body was.

From that point on, I decided I would at least go out once a day for fast food at the drive thru. I forced myself to get up. I threw on a hat and got dressed. I wore the same clothes repeatedly (Ewe!). One day I pulled my hair back and had the audacity to go to my daughter's school to pick her up. I lied to the teacher of course; I told her I had the flu, since she had no problem holding back how terrible I looked. After that adventure, I felt justified to go back to bed.

I'm one who journals; it has always been a form of therapy for me. Basically, it's my way of talking to God and releasing everything. It's also a way of remembering things. Well, during this period, I refused to journal. I didn't want to talk. I was in a terrible funk.

My attitude was full of negativity. I thrived on sarcasm. I had a nasty attitude about life in general. I refused to go to work. I refused to receive phone calls. When the telephone rang, I looked at the caller I.D. and depending on who was calling, I would either get angry, or cry, and throw the phone across the bed.

Two calls got through, by no fault of my own. Before I knew it, the phone was at my ear. Oh they had never heard me this way before. I was angry that

I was given the phone, and my attitude reflected it. I answered the phone, "What Do You Want!" My poor brother was calm, and so concerned. He tried to understand and figure out what was wrong, and why I felt the way I did. I laugh now, but it wasn't funny then. My sister said, "you're scaring me!" I think I yelled something like, "What are you scared about! Hey, to live is Christ and to die is gain!" It actually felt good lashing out.

One of those days I was watching T.V. and I found myself yelling back at the T.V. It appeared everything that came on aggravated me. The soaps were portraying Dracula. There were episodes of people arguing. People were conniving. They plotted, schemed, cheated, and it all frustrated me even more. Then, the thought actually hit me; I needed to get out of that bed. I felt like I was actually going to die if I stayed in bed. I said to myself, "this bed is trying to kill me." It was sucking me in. I felt like I was going straight through the mattress. Still angry as ever, and bitter, I knew I couldn't take my life. That was just unacceptable. I knew Satan couldn't take my life either. Mentally, I was at a crossroad. I didn't like how I felt physically as I laid in bed, nor did I want to get up and face the world.

Finally, I had a heart to heart with God. Yeah, He already knew what I was thinking and what I was going through. He knew me even before I was formed in my mother's womb. He knows the hairs on my head. He knew how I felt. But still, I had to use my words. I had to let the words come out of my mouth. I had to communicate my concerns. Everything comes back to the spoken word. Remember, God spoke things into existence. In the beginning was the Word, and the Word was with God, and the Word was God, and the Word became flesh and dwelled among the earth. Do you see the importance of words?

I talked to God and explained to him how I felt, all the pain, hurt, lack of respect, the whole nine yards. I was sitting in the living room on the floor in the dark, and it was as if we were in the future, as if I had already committed suicide. God told me I was five minutes away. He was saying I only had five minutes to go, and everything would have been over. Now I'm thinking, you mean I gave up, taking my life and I only had five more minutes to go. Then, I was back in the present, and I remember angrily saying to God, "five minutes! How long is five minutes?! Okay God." I thought to myself, fine, I'll give it a try. I wouldn't want to give up when I'm so close to a breakthrough.

From that point on, I went through a crying phase. I'm talking about being drenched with tears. Though I whimpered daily, I was always being comforted by God. Everywhere I looked, God was speaking. The more I saw and heard God, the more I cried. He was always speaking, but I wasn't always listening. If I were in the bedroom with the T.V. on, God talked to me through the TV. I was watching the worship channel and I remember so vividly, the man (worship leader) literally faced me and talked directly to me. It was like for a moment, he turned from the actual program to talk to me. He said, this type of depression ended only through praise and worship, and I had to praise my way through. When he said that, I began crying again. Sometimes it's hard to muster up praise when you're depressed, but I was determined. I cried, and praised profusely.

I remember driving and listening to Kirk Franklin's CD. I was singing the lyrics, "I know that I can make it, I know that I can stand, no matter what may come my way, my life is in your hands." I tried with everything in me to praise my way through. I chanted like a Native American. I was like a wounded bird trying to fly again. I knew God was ministering to me through that song. I knew he was carrying me.

God continued to reach out to me. Another evening I was driving, and as I stopped at a red light, I looked up to the sky and saw the clouds moving. God said, "See, I'm moving." That was confirmation to me that He was working my situation out. Hearing from God, feeling his touch, being consoled, and still I couldn't shake what I was feeling. I still couldn't stop crying. So I decided to hit the road.

A long ride down 95 South will soothe anybody's heart. The ride gave me time to clear my mind. I didn't know where I wanted to go or when I was coming back. But I knew I didn't want to talk to anyone. So that ruled out my parent's house.

As I drove down south, God allowed me to be alone with Him and my thoughts. He ministered to me through the trees. I wanted to go to the mountains, but I ended up at my parent's house after all. My mom just kept asking, "What's going on?" "Is everything okay?" "Why are you here?" I stuck to my guns. I replied, "Can't I visit?" "I'm on vacation."

"I'm taking a break." But momma wouldn't let up; she knew something was wrong. Finally, she let it go, but in her heart, she knew something was up.

Momma asked me to come sit on her bed and talk to her. I did reluctantly, but we didn't talk about me. She wanted me to pray about a situation with her. I kept saying to myself, "I'm not feeling this." Though she was animate about it, she said if you don't want to, don't. Well after that, I felt I had to pray. I guess I learned to pray in season and out of season.

My mom and I are a lot alike. We have the same body shape. Our personalities resemble each other, and so of course, we tend to clash sometimes. I was always a daddy's girl. But I have a lot of my mom's habits, some I like, and some I could do without. No offense mom. I love and appreciate my mom. She has always been there for me. She has always made many sacrifices for me and my sisters and brothers. I'm ever grateful for her and to her. She has a lot of wisdom to share, based on her own life. But sometimes you just don't want to hear, you need to do this or that, and I certainly didn't want any pity. To tell the truth, I no longer knew what I wanted.

That day, God used my mom in a mighty way without me saying a word. She began sharing all this stuff about her life and life in general. It really touched my heart. She was honestly relating to a lot of what I was dealing with. Sometimes we think our parents just don't understand. I was thinking to myself; she really gets it.

As we stood outside in the front yard beside the

tree she planted when I was a little girl, God allowed the sun to shine down on her. The glow coming from her skin was radiant. It was beautiful. I could feel the warmth coming from her heart. From that day forward, I saw her in a totally new light in more ways than one. (Thanks Momma). In a sense it was like running home crying, I want my momma, and finding her standing there with arms outstretched, waiting to receive me.

Getting back to suicide. Did you know some people can't even phantom how you get to the point of contemplating taking your life? Well I say to them, Bless God. But I also say if you've never experienced a thing, most likely you can't relate to or help someone else in that predicament.

On another note, your life is so precious. Nothing (no pressures of this world, no situation, no devastations, no failure, no missed opportunities, no tragedy) and no one (not your parents, your friends, your enemies, your family, your husband, wife, boyfriend, girlfriend, child or employer) is worth you ever even considering taking/ending your life.

God is the creator, the giver of life. Don't treat your life as if it means nothing. God created you, and he will carry you home at the appointed time. You're supposed to be like Jesus, and it wasn't suicide with Jesus. Jesus said no man take my life, but I lay it down, only to pick it back up again. You're like Jesus but you're not Jesus. You can't pick your life back up again, so don't allow wickedness or setbacks to convince you to give your life up.

You don't know what happens to you when you

95

decide to take your own life. You don't know what takes place between you killing yourself and meeting God. You don't understand the importance of your life. You don't see the potential you have. Your life is not your own. Your life is to glorify God and help others. What good are you dead? There's still going to come a day when you stand before God, and answer for your lack of trust in Him.

I think giving in to suicide is allowing someone or something to force you into defeat. You're saying it's too hard for you and it's certainly too hard for God. So you take matters into your own hands. Extreme measures! What happened to trusting in God? When you trust God, He will supply your every need. He'll place that someone there for you to confide in. You are never void of God's love. Don't throw in the towel. You are the recipient of God's favor. Life is short, too short to be depressed. As Bobby McFerrin puts it, "Don't Worry, Be Happy."

You were created for a purpose. Your life has meaning. Your life can bless, or encourage the lives of others.

10

Laughter

❦

A **time to weep and a time to laugh; a time to mourn, and a time to dance. (Ecclesiastes 3:4 KJV)** Finally, the laughter came. God must have been tickling me because I was laughing at silly things. Things that weren't normally funny to me, I laughed at, and it felt good. I've been told that I have dry wit; one person even said dried up wit. But I was laughing up a storm. People looked at me strangely and I didn't care; my joy had been restored.

Every episode of Fresh Prince had me in stitches. On the metro, people's mere expressions made me laugh. One of my co-workers kept me laughing. I know she probably thinks she's in the wrong profession as hard as I laughed at what she said. Even today she's funny, but I wouldn't go as far as comedian material.

I often quote, "the joy of the Lord is my strength." I know that to be more than just a quote now. I laughed so much until my heart was glad, thankful, and ever so grateful to God. I thanked God for bringing me out of darkness and into his marvelous light. Thank God for laughter. Laughter makes a merry heart.

See, I was oh too familiar with depression and suicide attempts. I'd been there and done that twice before. But let me just tell you, you have to die to those stages of defeat. Each time you escape and allow yourself to be placed in either pit again, the pit only gets deeper. It gets harder to climb out. That's why some people don't make it out. But with God, nothing is impossible.

Please don't fall prey to those strongholds. If you are in that pit now, get out! Determine in your heart not to go back, ever. I promised God with everything in me that I would not fall into depression ever again, nor would I allow suicidal thoughts to enter my mind again. You have to control your thoughts, **casting down imaginations, and every high thing that exalteth itself against the knowledge of God, and bringing into captivity every thought to the obedience of Christ. (2 Corinthians 10:5 KJV)**

You have to let your mind dwell on things that are positive. **Finally, brethren, whatever is true, whatever is honorable, whatever is right, whatever is pure, whatever is lovely, whatever is of good repute, if there is any excellence and if anything worthy of praise, let your mind dwell on these things. (Philippians 4:8 NAS)**

Day by day God renewed my strength. He truly lifted the Spirit of heaviness from me. I admitted,

"God, I have to really die now. I have to change. I have to trust that you know what's best for me. I vowed, God I'll throw myself into You, into your Word. You're all I have. You're the very air I breathe. In you there's laughter. Because of you, I can laugh again."

Laughing is good for the Soul.

11

Rejoice

❧

I WILL praise thee, O LORD, with my whole heart; I will show forth all thy marvelous works. I will be glad and rejoice in thee: I will sing praise to thy name, O thou most High. (Psalm 9:1-2 KJV) I laughed right on into praise and worship. Hallelujah! Thank you Jesus. Each day God allowed me to see, I rejoiced and was glad.

And we also have joy with our troubles because we know that these troubles produce patience. And patience produces character, and character produces hope. (Romans 5:3-4 NCV) God is using life's difficulties and Satan's attack to build our character. For without testing, we would never know what we are capable of doing, nor would we grow. Without the refining we will not become more pure and more like Christ.

Great is thy faithfulness, morning by morning new mercies I see, all I have needed thy hand hath provided. (I bare witness to God's faithfulness. I saw his new mercies daily in my life. I bare witness to his provisions of all I needed and desired. I witnessed the reality of restoration).

I will bless the Lord at all times, (not just when things are going well). His praise shall continually be in my mouth, (regardless to what the situation looks like). My soul shall make her boast in the Lord, the humble shall hear thereof and be glad. Oh, magnify the Lord with me and let us exalt His name together. I sought the Lord and He heard me and delivered me from all my fears. (I am ever grateful. I have been delivered).

I will lift up mine eyes to the hills from whence cometh my help. My help cometh from the Lord. (I trust God to deliver me through whatever suffering afflicts me, no matter its severity. He is my source. He is my strength. I will rejoice forevermore).

Though Satan may be trying to run rampant in your life, Jesus came that we might have life, and life more abundantly, and we shall. Put on the garment of praise. Get Radical. Break a Sweat. Shout with a Loud Exuberant Voice. Exercise those vocal cords, I dare you!

Do a dance- A holy dance. I remember I told God I wanted to dance before Him like David did. I mean I didn't want to dance out of my clothes or anything. I just wanted to give Him my all through dance. I visited my sister's church one night. I didn't want to go. I wasn't feeling up to it. But she insisted. She even picked me up. The theme was along the lines of "Dance like David did." I started off clowning, acting like the comedian Martin Lawrence when he dances.

Then before I knew it, I took off running around the church. It was a somewhat awkward feeling, but I went with it. After I ran around the church, I remember asking, "God, what do I do now?" All of a sudden, I was popping like MC Hammer and sliding like James Brown. I screamed out of shock. It seemed the more I screamed, the faster my legs moved. I went from one end of the church to the other end in a flash. It was like a fire, a surge, electricity shooting through my body.

It was off the hook, like young folk say, "off the heezy" "off the hizzle fo shizzle," okay one more, "off the chain." But then I danced until I was practically out of breath. I danced until I coughed. I danced until I frowned. I danced until I literally wanted to cry. Not only was my body's movement being controlled, Mother nature was visiting, and I was not physically fit. I was telling God, "That's enough! You can stop now!" But he wouldn't stop.

Although you don't control your speed, I pray the next time I get that fire shut up in my bones, I'll be in better shape. That's a true work out. Bally's ain't got nothing on that one. Be sure you want what you ask for. I'm a firm believer, if you A.S.K. you will G.E.T.

Listen. However you rejoice really doesn't matter, just rejoice in the Lord. I refuse to minimize your pain, but if you maximize your faith and trust in the Lord, *get a promise, wait on the Lord, deny yourself, get a glimpse of death, see the glory of the Lord, go through the healing process, surrender,*

be aware of the tactics of the enemy, don't get caught up in worldly things, conquer the stages of defeat, learn to laugh, and rejoice in the Lord, then victory is yours!

You Can Die! And Stay Dead!

DEAD WOMAN WALKING!

12

So I thought...

⟋⟋∾⟍⟍

Death is never easy. There's a grieving process, and it's okay to grieve, but know that God is our comforter. Trouble doesn't last always. Weeping may endure for a night, but joy comes in the morning. Don't allow anything to stand in the way of your morning.

Overall, I died many times, meaning, I denied my flesh often. But, I didn't know how to stay dead. I didn't know how to keep my flesh under submission. I kept crawling off the altar. I kept giving my concerns to God and taking them back, and as a result, the unthinkable happened.

13

Crawling off the Altar

Repeated cycles got me down, and I was tired of experiencing the same old results. I wanted different results. When I didn't see things change fast enough, I sometimes lost my cool. As a result of going through the same thing over and over again, I was affected physically. Migraines set in. I use to have migraines so bad that whenever I was stressed, concerned, annoyed, or frustrated, I was sure to be hit right between the eyes. Sometimes, the pain would even take a rapid turn, hitting me in the left eye with a force that could have moved a building. The pain shifted around my head like it owned me.

Over time, God delivered me from migraines. Now when I was stressed and out of control emotionally, excruciating pain went straight to my stomach. I think I would have preferred the migraines to what I was about to encounter. I was walking around looking like a corpse. Dark circles claimed residence under my eyes. My stomach hurt so bad I could barely walk. It took a lot of energy and effort to walk. I was struggling to not fall. I doubled over with pain. My stomach felt very heavy, and it felt like it was pulling downward. I was weak. It hurt to talk. The repeated cycles were whipping me.

It was obvious. I was dying, but not to sin. I was dying because of sin. God said get rid of anger and rage, but I was holding on to it. It was trying desperately to take me down. The heartache I felt, the pounding of my heart, along with the frustration were turning me into a helpless pit of anger, rage, and bitterness all because of where my personal life was headed, because of the betrayal I felt, and because of the helpless state I felt I had been thrown into.

I had a tremendous urge to cry but there was a part of me that wouldn't allow me to cry. When I was in a public place, the tears attempted to seep out. I kept pushing the tears back until finally, they forced their way to the forefront. Eventually, I gave in, but within seconds, the tears ceased. This continued to happen, and each time I was left with a burning sensation in my stomach that came and went. Thank God He doesn't allow us to be consumed with grief or nonsense.

Finally, when I did cry, I cried, "My God! My God! I know you haven't forsaken me. I know you're with me." The cycles I experienced were sometimes overwhelming. I could see them coming but I didn't have a grip on them. If I planned a proper response to the cycle, it appeared I still got knocked down occasionally. If I ignored the cycles, it appeared I was still trampled upon. If I acted like a mad woman because of the cycles, things appeared to get worse. I cried, "Lord Jesus, what else can I do? Though you slay me, yet will I trust you."

God was telling me, "first, stop taking matters into your own hands. Stop giving me your cares and taking them back. Stop consuming yourself with prayer one minute and anger the next. Stop coming to me broken and after I've replenished you, you go back to the same old attitude or state of mind. You can't do this alone. You can't change anything or anyone, but I can."

My best friend told me she didn't know what kind of heart I had to endure so much. I always felt better after talking to her. She even made me laugh at my trials as devastating as they were. She applauded my strength. God, I applauded my strength. But I couldn't take credit. It was God's strength in me. I always knew, to whom much was given, much was required. My feelings were, "WOW! I'm getting an awful lot after this ordeal. Abundance I'd say."

Thinking this way helped me more than it hurt. So, I guess all this meant I was numb, but not dead. I hadn't completely died to the old way of responding to my problems. I pleaded, "God you've got to embalm me this time. It takes a lot of energy, and it's too painful to get back up. Help me to die. Help me Lord! Step in. Reach in and pronounce me dead. Help me to do it your way so that it won't hurt so badly. Help me to do it your way, so that I'll get it right and move pass this."

I thought I was beyond letting things get to me.

My body was tired, sluggish-like. My appetite came and went, but my weight increased. I was waking to hot sweats. I had diarrhea. My peace was floating around somewhere in the air. My joy was on the top shelf. I was struggling to hold on. But I was saved. I was going to heaven. Often, I yelled out to Satan. "At least I'm not going to hell. You're a defeated foe. Your final destination is Hell." That gave me comfort, even though my life was still in shambles.

Then God told me, **"For a long time I have kept silent, I have been quiet and held myself back. But now, like a woman in child birth, I cry out, I gasp and pant. I will lay waste the mountains and hills and dry up all their vegetation; I will turn rivers into islands and dry up the pools. I will lead the blind by ways they have not known, along unfamiliar paths I will guide them; I will turn darkness into light before them and make the rough places smooth. These are the things I will do; I will not forsake them. But those who trust in idols, who say to images, 'You are our gods,' will be turned back in utter shame. (Isaiah 42:14-17 NIV)**

I thank God that He comes to our rescue continuously. I thank him that He never gave up on me. Just as I had to learn to do, Trust God with all of your affairs. Sure it's hard. But it's even harder trying to take matters in your own hands. Stop going through the same old repeated cycles. If you keep doing the same thing, you will keep getting the same results, or eventually worse results. A lot of my pain was unnecessary. I focused too much on me. I concentrated more on my feelings, than on God, the one who gave me those emotions.

Are you experiencing unnecessary pain? Are you giving your cares to God and then taking them back? If doing it your way hasn't worked all these years, that should tell you something. Put it on the altar and leave it there. Lay prostrate before God and allow Him to hover over you. Allow him to do some major surgery on you. He will sanctify you, but it's a process. That process begins with your heart, a right attitude, and the Altar.

14

Separation

❧

**So they are no longer two but one flesh.
What therefore God has joined together, let
no man put asunder. (Matthew 19:6 AB)**

"God, this must be it. I must be closer to my
promise. Things must be getting ready to
turn around. God it hurts. I'm having mixed feelings. I'm kind of excited because I feel something
good has to come out of this separation. Wait a
minute. Have I failed you Lord? I feel down, and sad
as if I disappointed you."

"Should I have done more? I know I could have.
I see my faults now. Things are clear now. But God I
don't want to go back to the way it use to be. In my
heart, I know this separation isn't permanent. I know
things will change. I just don't know when."

Separations are painful for both mates involved
in some form or another. But depending on the

circumstances, a set aside period of time can also be healthy. No, I'm not promoting separation by any means. If you're the type who like being married, separation can be a long, dark and lonely time. I think you both eventually see that the grass isn't greener on the other side. Always, let the Spirit lead you in decision making. What works for me may not work for you. No two situations are the same.

We all have free will. We have choices in life. We can't control another human. God our creator doesn't try to step in and control our every move. He gives us a choice. He doesn't bombard us, nor does He force himself on us. So that ought to give us an inkling that we have no control over anyone.

It took me a long time to understand that you have to release individuals. You know the expression, "if you love something set it free, and if it comes back, it was meant to be." In other words, what will be, will be. We can't afford to be hindrances in the lives of others, especially spiritually.

In the early stages of my separation, I felt like I was in a big hole. No matter how I tried to close it, it remained open. No matter how hard I tried to climb out, I just couldn't. Only God could fill that hole, that void. I knew there was no emptiness or lack in God. I knew I needed to use my separation period to draw even closer to God. Where else could I turn?

As I yielded my spirit, my will to God, little by little, He began to close that hole. I got myself in position to be used and glorified by God. I made some much needed changes, some major and some minor. I finally did all the things I hadn't had time to do. I used my time wisely, doing constructive things.

Although I had even more on my plate and constantly felt the pressure, I was determined to make God proud of my life. Satan was in trouble now. He tried to tear me away from my father, but instead I craved God even more. God was my hope, my strength, my provider. He sustained me. He was my all, even in this. My relationship with God became more intimate.

People sort of left me. They had their own agendas. The phone didn't ring as much. It was as if folk were distant all of a sudden. It was even like, my situation was a joke to some. I certainly wasn't on their minds anymore.

I didn't share with many people, but the ones who knew weren't there. But it just motivated me more. I realized once again, when you're hanging out there on some lim, most people will leave you hanging there. My advice to others has always been to follow your heart. If you're not ready to move forward, you won't do it successfully. You have to do what you know you can handle at that moment. Don't allow just anybody to influence you. They won't always be there when it counts, when you need them. But God will never leave nor forsake you.

In my personal experience, people were fast to offer opinions and comments, but when I looked up, all I saw was the residue left from their words. When it boiled down to it, it was just me and God. My advice to you is take your instructions from God. He won't turn away. He has your best interest at heart.

I knew I needed to clean up my surrounding, and

I knew I needed cleansing on the inside as well. During my time of cleaning and cleansing, I asked God to give me a new perspective. **James 1:21-27 advises us to get rid of all that is wrong in our lives.** I wanted to do just that. I wanted to think differently, act differently and do differently. I wanted God's mind set. I wanted to live my life God's way. I wanted to please God, not man. I also wanted to prove to people that regardless to what I endured, I would still serve God.

We have to always remember that though we're often separated from people, things, or the familiar and comfortable, nothing can separate us from the love of God. **Who shall ever separate us from Christ's love? Shall suffering and affliction and tribulation? Or calamity and distress? Or persecution, or hunger, or destruction, or peril or sword? For I am persuaded beyond doubt – am sure – that neither death, nor life, nor angels, nor principalities, nor things impending and threatening, nor things to come, nor powers, nor height, nor depth, nor anything else in all creation will be able to separate us from the love of God which is in Christ Jesus our Lord. (Romans 8:35,38-39 AB)**

As I drew closer to God, realizing I would never be separated from his love, things became more bearable. I was able to see some of the things that needed to take place in order to end my separation. I was also able to see all of the unrighteous behavior I had contributed to the relationship.

15

Ride the Storm

❧

"Lord, I feel good. I mean things aren't the way I want them, nor is it what I anticipated. But I'm riding the storm. You're carrying me like never before. I can't believe how good I feel. I'm smiling, and I feel good about myself. I can sleep at night. My stomach doesn't hurt anymore. My heart doesn't feel broken."

"The pain is gone." It's like having a baby and when the contractions hit, the impact almost knock the breath out of you. But once you get that epidermal, the contractions are still coming with the same force, but you don't feel them. "God I feel like I could stay here for a while. Just take your time. This feels good. But please don't take your hand off me."

"I'm able to encourage people who are going through the very thing that besets me. I don't know how long I'll be in this state, but I know you're working on my behalf. I know the end result will be glorious. I know you've transition me from a wreck to stability in you."

"People who know of my storm are questioning my strength. They wonder what I'm operating under, but I know it's you, Lord. I know it's your grace, your love and your mercy. Family members think I'm crazy. They think I'm taking this faith thing a little too far. They think I want this so badly that I'm dreaming it. But God, you know that it is the hope I have in you, according to your Word, that keeps me standing."

"I'm happy in you Lord. I'm no longer angry. I'm no longer holding on to the past. I'm still standing. I still have my self-esteem. I'm still able to do what you require of me. People don't understand. They aren't relating to me now. God, my prayer is that you don't allow anyone who knows about my storm to die until he/she sees the manifestation of your promise in my life. All these people who are mocking my faith, let them all see. For them, seeing is believing, but I have your promise. I stand on what you say and not what I see." One of my sisters said I have the gift of faith. Well I know the just shall live by their faith. I know **when we believe that God will fulfill his promises though we don't see them materializing, we demonstrate true faith. (John 20:24-31).**

I can't believe that my situation remains the same, but yet I feel so good. "God, I know the storm is almost done. I can see the sun peeping through the clouds. I have your promise before me. I can hear you clearly. I'm open to do your perfect will. I pray for peace, joy and your grace and mercy for my husband. Please don't take your hand off him either. Protect him, Lord. Mend his heart, Lord, as you have mended mine. Lord I'm your vessel. What would you have me to do Father?"

"Huh! Did you say let's talk about forgiveness? (Seen and Unseen). Lord, I didn't think I had a problem with forgiveness. I thought we cleared that up a long time ago. I thought I was very good at repenting and asking forgiveness."

Though we may think some things are unrelated, they are all linked together. With God every thing works together. Every thing has relevance.

"What's that God? You want me to actually stand before this person and ask forgiveness?

Oh my goodness!"

God said, "Yes, Who are you to judge anyone? I am God. Repent."

I stood before this person and pronounced judgement. Therefore, I had to stand before this person and ask forgiveness. I prejudged a person when told about a particular issue. Always keep in mind, God sees all and knows all, and we don't have the right to prejudge.

The bible talks about, he who is without sin, cast the first stone. I don't think any of us can pick up that stone. The bible also talks about vengeance is the Lord's, and He will repay. That tells me that we ought to continue in obedience, showing forth love, and trusting God to judge and punish accordingly. Besides, do you know if you prejudge, you will one day answer to God, and answer for the very act of judging. God forbid if your accusations against someone are false.

You know it amazing how we're quick to accuse others of unthinkable things, but yet we don't want to be accused of anything. I had forgotten what it felt like to be on the other end. I had forgotten, I knew the devastating effect of being falsely accused of a gruesome thing. False accusations do something inside a person. Not only does it hurt, it tears down and destroys. It even makes you question how people could possibly look at you that way. It's not just the false accusation that immobilizes you, it's the thought of the very act that eats at your heart.

Have you ever been falsely accused of something that you thought was so far fetched from your character? Although the accusation is false, it's hard to get beyond the very thought. We use to say, sticks and stones may break my bones, but words will never hurt. We know that's not true. Life and Death are in the power of the tongue. Negative, evil, talk cannot only ruin reputations, but lower self-esteems and put people in bondage.

"Okay Lord, I learned a valuable lesson about judging others." I humbly asked the person to forgive me, and I was forgiven. Thank God. The person accepted my apology. "Thank you God that the division that tried to come between this person and me can no longer bridge a gap."

"What did you say God? I'm not done with Forgiveness? There's someone else?

God I'm waiting for this huge apology, and you're telling me I have to apologize. I don't get it."

I was expecting an apology for all the wrong I thought my husband had done. But I didn't think I owed him an apology for all the wrong I had done. I quickly learned in order to be used as a vessel for God, you have to come clean in every area.

"God I think I should be on the receiving end this time. This is awful humbling."

I had an almost choked up effect with having to give this apology. It was humbling. I felt I had been wronged. But God was telling me, I had an ought against my husband, and I knew my husband had an ought against me. He was telling me to go ask my husband forgiveness. I figured I'm always asking forgiveness even when I'm not wrong. This time he was going to apologize, and I wouldn't budge until he did. After all, I wasn't wrong.

Finally, giving in to God, I agreed to ask forgiveness, not knowing God would give me a list of things to ask forgiveness for. He took me way back to the beginning of our marriage. Good Gracious! I thought I would never get through that list. I had a lot of stuff to be forgiven for. No wonder we had so many issues. Mrs. Holy-Roller needed to come clean. I was so caught up in keeping track of my husband's wrong, I forgot I was just as wrong. I thought I was the better Christian. NOT.

I humbled myself, and I was obedient to God. I asked forgiveness for my wrong with a sincere heart. First, I asked God to forgive me. Then, I asked my husband to forgive me. It turns out, my husband had already asked me to forgive him, but I couldn't hear his apology. It was at a time when all I heard were negative thoughts, and I wouldn't have believed he was sincerely apologetic anyway.

After apologizing, I felt free. I felt light. I felt joyous. I felt a sigh of relief. I even smiled. When my heart was finally open to receive my husband's apology, I heard it clearly, and I received it. Then, not only did I apologize for my wrongdoing, but I was lead to make confessions. My husband quickly forgave me of all I asked forgiveness for.

Sometimes we don't know what it means to obey God wholeheartedly, but the truth will always set us free. I was free, indeed. There were no secrets, no skeletons, no unresolved issues causing stress on my behalf. Everything was out in the open for me, and as a result, healing could take place, mending could begin.

After those two hurdles, I figured, I could forgive anybody, or ask anybody to forgive me. Hallelujah! I had successfully moved pass the unforgiving stage for now. I asked forgiveness and both individuals forgave me. Do you know how that feels? Truly it's an amazing feeling. I felt like a new person. I was excited. I felt a weight had been lifted. Afterwards, God used me to speak to others about Forgiveness and Trusting only in Him. Hum! You can't be a witness if you're not first a partaker.

Now, hear me. It's easy to die/denying yourself, taking up your cross daily and following God when the problem or situation isn't before you when it's been removed. God told me to ask my husband to come back, and then die. He said, "End your separation, and then die to your flesh." In other words, stay the course, and learn to die while in your present situation in spite of what you're going through. Endure the suffering. Your suffering is not in vain.

16

Illusion of Pride

**I will break down your stubborn pride
and make the sky above you like iron and
the ground beneath you like bronze.
(Leviticus 26:19 NIV)**

Sometimes in life even as Christians, we become
more high minded than we ought to. We take on
the attitude that we're better than others and even
holier than others. The bible talks about such self-
righteous attitudes. It tells us that even when we
think we're doing right, we sin, falling short of the
Glory of God. Our goodness is as filthy rags.

Before we attempt to elevate ourselves or allow
anyone else to put us on a pedestal, we should all
take to heart, **for it is by grace you have been
saved, through faith – and this not from yourselves, it is the gift of God – not by works, so that
no one can boast. (Ephesians 2:8-9 NIV)** Salvation

is a gift from God to all who will receive it. This gift is not based on the things we do. (Church attendance, charitable contributions, tithing, etc., does not save us).

How can we afford to be puffed up with pride?

A man's pride brings him low, but a man of lowly spirit gains honor. (Proverbs 29:23 NIV)

Don't think because you go through the motions of going to church, tithing, and occasionally praising God that you're better than the next person. Remember when Jesus talked about the hypocrites, the lukewarm folks, He said He'd spue them out of his mouth. God wants us all to be either hot or cold. There is no room for in between. If you're full of pride, you're in between.

We are to use our gifts to uplift and encourage others, not to display arrogance. We're all given different gifts and talents. We are all called to many different things, but none of us, or our gifts, are higher than the other. We are not to exalt ourselves.

To fear the Lord is to hate evil; I hate pride and arrogance, evil behavior and perverse speech. (Proverbs 8:13 NIV) Not only is thinking you're the better Christian a form of pride, but so is racism. Remember Noah from the Old Testament? Well, he had three sons, Shem, Ham and Japheth. From those three sons came people who were scattered over the earth. (All people, all nationalities). So that tells me, no race is better than the other. **From one blood God**

created all nations to dwell among the earth. God created us all equally and in his image. He loves us all the same. Will you choose to die to racism? Cast down the thoughts that come to your mind about another race. Allow God to renew your mind?

Pride goes before destruction, a haughty spirit before a fall. (Proverbs 16:18 NIV)

Looking down on people will always come back to haunt you. You've climbed up the ladder of success in your eyes, and so you discount the very people who helped you get your start.

I had to humble myself going back to thank the people who took me in, the people who gave me a place to stay, food to eat, and a job, while pushing me to be better. What did they ask for in return? Nothing. Sometimes we aren't as appreciative as we ought to be. But reflect back to all you have because of your humble beginning.

Because of the people who gave me my start, doors were open that may not have otherwise been opened to me. I know I would not have moved from down south to Maryland. I would most likely still be living in my hometown. I would not have the current job I have. There weren't much opportunity job wise. I know I wouldn't have half the experiences and eye openers that city life has afforded me. All of my experiences weren't pleasant, but they were learning experiences. I would not have met my husband of more than fourteen years. I would not have the daughter I was blessed to have by him.

God brought these things to my remembrance, and I had to deal with them all. Some of us are prone to get amnesia. Have you been blessed for so long, that you can no longer relate to people less fortunate than you? That's a bad place to be. No one is asking you to trade places with anyone less fortunate than you. What I'm saying is, you can't get so lost in your accomplishments or success that you're no longer sensitive to the needs of others.

• **Memory Lane**

I eat very well now, sometimes a little too well, but I remember eating mustard sandwiches when I moved out on my own. I remember it being a challenge to buy tomatoes and tuna.

I dress pretty decently now, and shop frequently, but I can remember wearing hand-me-downs. Back in 1978-1979 even before a tragic house fire, as a child, we wore hand-me-downs. Losing all you own in a house fire, and having only the clothes on your back is devastating. But for me, there was still that ounce of pride, having to wear my classmates clothes to school the day after I received them.

I have running water now, and inside plumbing, but I remember using the outdoor toilet, and having to heat water for baths.

I have a telephone now, but I remember growing up without a phone in the house, and not learning how to use one until I was 18. I also remember living on my own and having my service temporarily disconnected due to lack of payment.

I have a car now, and I have had several cars, but

I remember having to walk to church, and I didn't mind it.

I have a job that I enjoy going to now, but I remember when I didn't look forward to getting up at 6:00 a.m. and riding on the back of a truck to go pull tobacco. It was cold and wet in the mornings. Dew was still on the tobacco. We dressed with several layers of old clothing because the tobacco easily stained them. As time quickly passed, it got very hot and humid, and our clothes were dirty and they felt sticky. Tobacco worms the size of Vienna sausages were relaxing on the leaves of practically every other stalk of tobacco. We worked at a fast pace as to not be there all day, and it was torture on our backs. The tobacco stained our nails, and left our bodies smelly and soiled. The pay wasn't even minimum wage, but it was a job. I was lucky to make $17 a day. It's a glorious thing to go from $17 a day to more than $17 an hour.

I have a greater appreciation for my floor now. I don't mind laying prostrate before God on the floor. I can freely kneel on the floor, or just sit there for long periods of time. I can even walk around bare feet with ease. But I remember a time when I wouldn't dare do any of that because mice, and roaches ruled my domicile.

I have many rooms now, but I remember renting a room with no window, paying $200 a month. I could never tell if it was day or night without going outside. The so-called window I thought I had was boarded up. It turned out, the boarded area was the entrance to another room that was rented out as well. Because there was not a window, I had to use a humidifier to create some type of moisture in the room.

I have tons of toilet paper now, I even personally use a roll a day, but I remember using newspaper and rags instead.

I said all that to say, remember, you are where you are today by the grace of God. God wants us to trade our pride for his humility.

I have never gone to a professional wrestling or boxing arena, but I witnessed the violence weekly. The impact was so great that for a long time, I thought when I got to the point of anger, and could no longer adequately express my feelings, it was okay to start punching and using vulgar language.

I use to watch "Cops", "bad boys, bad boys, whatcha gonna do, whatcha gonna do when they come for you." I thought nothing of it when I saw scenes of domestic violence. I saw people crying, "I didn't do anything." Then one day, I found myself in the middle of a domestic dispute, wondering if I was on candid camera, and crying, "but I didn't do anything."

Maybe you can't relate to any of these things. Or maybe you simply forgot some of these things. Maybe you escaped this lifestyle. Maybe you lived a sheltered life. But some of us were not as fortunate. You never know the wounds an individual carries. You don't know the hidden pain. You never know what an individual has endured or what scars that person bares. So before you turn your nose up, consider the fact that it could have easily been you to bear their cross.

Ask God to show you how to relate to others.

Ask God to show you how to get rid of pride. Maybe you can't relate to abuse, and your questions are many concerning abuse. Be careful not to stand in judgment of what you don't know or can't relate to. There's a possibility that the very thing you judge will present itself in your family one day. Does it have to hit home for you to feel the extent of the scrutiny?

Release the Pride. Step into Humility.

17

A New Life

See I am doing a new thing! Now it springs up; do you not perceive it? I am making a way in the desert and streams in the wasteland. (Isaiah 43:19 NIV)

Praise be to God! Finally, I'm experiencing a life I have yearned for. My marriage is sweet. It's lovely. It's heavenly. Things around me are going well. It's not because of me but because of God's glory. Pinch me. Am I dreaming? God is this really happening? I'm finally seeing the abundant life here on earth. I have a glow as a pregnant woman. Can my love grow any deeper for this man? He use to sometimes treat me like a Princess, now he's treating me like a Queen. Oh, I'm just ecstatic.

I always knew your word would not return unto you void, but it would accomplish what you sent it to do. You said, don't grow weary in well doing, but in due season I would reap if I fainted not. And I'm finally reaping. All the years of hoping for something, believing for something, receiving it, and then finally, seeing it manifested in the natural. It was manifested in the Spirit realm long ago, and now finally, I can relax, relate, and release. I can Exhale.

Once God moves you to another level in Him, you've passed the test. You have a new life. Now, continue to speak those things that are not as though they were. Your mind set has changed. Don't allow it to be swayed. Stop trying to think the way you use to. Sometimes out of a negative habit, we react to situations strictly out of habit. Realize things are not the same. Your mind has been renewed. Ask God to help you keep that new mind set. Your life has changed. Things around you have changed. Remember you're the head and not the tail. You've been restored. You've been redeemed. Walk in your newness.

Stay in God's presence. He will hear your cry. **I waited patiently for the LORD; and he inclined unto me, and heard my cry. He brought me up also out of an horrible pit, out of the miry clay, and set my feet upon a rock, and established my goings. And he has put a new song in my mouth, even praise unto our God: many shall see it, and fear, and shall trust in the LORD. (Psalm 40:1-3 KJV)**

He truly sustained me. He gave me peace for tomorrow and He promises peace for you as well.

18

Temporary Set Back

❦

So we fix our eyes not on what is seen, but on what is unseen. For what is seen is temporary, but what is unseen is eternal. (2 Corinthians 4:18 NIV)

Have you ever loved someone so much that the things they did affected you to the point where you felt nothing but disgust and disappointment? "Lord, have Mercy! What do I do now?" As things began to take a turn, all I could do was laugh. No words could express how I felt. But I didn't have to try to make sense out of what was happening. God knew.

Sometimes people don't quite understand the deep hurt they cause you. Sometimes people underestimate your strengths and weaknesses. They don't realize the extent of your pain. Yolanda Adams sings, "This battle is not yours." These are not just words.

Truly it's not your battle. God wants to use us as his vessel. He wants to use us to touch the lives of others. He knows what we can handle, and what we can't. He allows us to go through storms for a reason. Look at it from the perspective of God using us to glorify Him through our humility and obedience.

Now, for the setback. Okay, so depression, loneliness, and suicidal thoughts are dead, they can't grip me anymore. The Stronghold has been broken. Praise be to God that alcohol, drugs, adultery and fornication died many years ago. "But God, what's this thing that keeps trying to pop up, not often, but often enough?" It's like a reminder of the bad experiences. Every time you think a particular issue is dead, it jumps up in your face in disguise saying, "Here I am." It's like Satan is saying, "You didn't think you would go scot-free, did you? Come on now, you know I have to annoy you with something. I really want to just destroy you."

So disappointment rears its ugly head. Broken promises are the root of your disappointment. The things you thought were a thing of the past have come back to haunt you. Now you have a choice, give in and go through all the turmoil again, or **press toward the mark for the prize of the high calling of God in Christ Jesus. (Philippians 3:14 KJV)**

Are you going to trust the one who broke the promise or the one who is the Promise keeper? Your Spirit is still willing to come under submission, but your flesh is weak. Deep down you're distraught, but you know God can handle this, too. Of course you can make it through this phase. You've been through worse. This phase should be a piece of cake with God's help.

The difficulty comes in because you're practically worn out from all the past drama. You're determined to not go back to Drama Land. The test comes because you've opened up your heart to trust again. Now, you have to decide what you're going to do. Are you going to sit back and feel the knife jabbing in your flesh again? Or are you going to refuse to be cut again? You've already been stabbed so many times that it's a wonder you still have flesh. Don't forget you're operating under a new mind set this time. Things aren't the way they seem. You still have to be willing to forgive over and over again. Are you suffering for God? If you are, His grace is sufficient for you in all areas of your life. He cares about disappointment too. You've already seen him at work.

The setback is temporary. It's designed to make you think things haven't changed. It's designed to make you think you labored in vain. It's designed to make you waver. Don't believe the hype. Satan is a liar. He is a deceiver. He wants to sift you as wheat, but the fight is over. The storm is over. No matter what it looks like, all you're really feeling is the debris that's left from the storm. Hold on my sister. Hold on my brother. You're coming down the stretch. Can't you see the flags at the finish line? Can't you hear the roaring of the crowd? Don't you hear the chanting? You made it! And you owe it all to God. NOW PRESS ON!

19

Clean Up Your Act

❧❦❧

We all need to stop and evaluate our way of living. We were not created to acquire stuff, travel, party, and then die. Author F.E. Marsh of the Discipler's Manual says, "we were created to serve God and to reconcile people to God by sharing the glorious news of God's love, that God saves people through His Son, the Lord Jesus Christ. God wants to reveal Himself to the world; He longs for all men to know Him, to know Him personally."

For we must all appear before the judgment seat of Christ; that every one may receive the things done in his body, according to that he hath done, whether it be good or bad. (2 Corinthians 5:10 KJV)

Author F.E. Marsh further says, "first the believer is to be made manifest at the judgment seat of Christ as he was known by the Lord in this present life. He said the revelation is this:

Ambitions that are not of the Lord will be revealed.

Black bitterness against others will be detected.

Covetousness of the heart will be unmasked.

Deviations from the truth will be discovered.

Envyings of others will become apparent.

Fault finding with our brethren will be discerned.

Grumblings and murmurings will be disclosed.

Heart backslidings and secret faults will be made known.

Indulgings of the flesh and selfishness will be unearthed.

Wrongful judging of others will be unfolded.

Love of money, ease and the world will be obvious.

Mixed motives in work for Christ will be ferreted out.

Opportunities lost for doing good and confessing Christ will be shown up.

Perverseness of heart and pleasures not of God will be evident.

Quarrellings, backbiting, anger and malice will be seen.

Rebelliousness under God's chastening hand will be distinguished.

Selfishness, slanderings, and self-will will be observed.

Tremblings before the world will be palpable.

Uncleanness of heart will be recognized.

Willfulness and wanderings will be visible.

We shall be heartily glad for the fire to burn up all this heap of rubbish and shall adoringly praise the Lord for his grace and love toward us. Second, the believer is to give an account of himself to the Lord as to his conduct towards fellow-believers. Third, believers will have the quality of their work judged."

So you see, we don't really get away with any thing. There is no escape from God. Clean up your act. Enough said.

20

A Cry for Help

⁌⋯⁖⋯⁍

Prayer is a powerful tool. It is a weapon designed for Christians. It is a source of communication between God the Father and us, his creation. It's communication between the Holy Spirit and the Father on our behalf. It's communication between God the Father and the Son, Jesus Christ on our behalf. Prayer is simply talking to God. Pouring out your concerns. Casting all your cares on the Lord. Seeking instruction.

Some people are confident that their prayers are being heard and answered. Others think because of their way of living, they can't get a prayer through. They think they aren't connected to God, and as a result, they are fooled into believing they would be wasting their time praying. Regardless to your state, I say pray anyway.

If my people, who are called by my name, will humble themselves and pray and seek my face

and turn from their wicked ways, then will I hear from heaven and will forgive their sin and will heal their land. (2 Chronicles 7:14 NIV) If you are a Christian, you need to be praying. Prayer changes things. God has given us the solution to much of the World's problems. But for some reason, we choose not to use his solution.

Why is the world in such a hostile state? It is because the Children of God are too tired, frustrated, busy, lazy or unequipped to pray. There are things that are dear to us that we're waiting for God to change. We want to see the change, yet we won't pray for that very thing to come to pass. We simply sit back and wish it would happen. Like I said before, everything comes back to the spoken word. God spoke things into existence, and He tells us to use his Word to do the same. Speak to your situation. Speak to your storm. Prophesy in his name.

When people asks for prayer, they are asking because they need the hand of God to move in their lives. I remember my husband use to do things that I wasn't pleased with. When I got upset, he would always say, I should pray instead of getting angry. He said as a Christian, even if I had to pray 365 times a day, I should do just that. It took me years to realize that those words were a plea for help. As long as I remained too angry to pray for him or us, things remained the same. When I finally got the revelation about prayer and prayed with a sincere heart, I began to see God working even faster in our lives.

I didn't want to exert the energy to pray he stopped doing things that angered me. I figured because I wanted him to stop, he should have stopped, or God should have made him stop. It took effort for me to pray. It didn't take any effort for me to want. Sometimes as humans, our flesh has such hold on us, and we allow our sin to have such control over us that it seems almost impossible to stop doing things that are wrong. But know that Jesus died for our sins and because of his shed blood, sin has no control over us. God has told us that we're more than conquerors through Jesus. Through prayer, we receive power from God to overcome any wrongdoing. Stop looking for the answer to your problem. You already have it. Now Pray.

Although we should pray for others, those in our household should be our top priority when we pray. We should always cover them in prayer. Sometimes it's easier to pray for those we don't know, or those we don't live with. What if when you get to judgment day, you find out that your prayer was the only prayer that went up on behalf of your family member? What if you find that no one is praying for your loved one? That would be a sad day.

What does it cost you to Pray? Will you respond to the cry for Help?

21

No Cross No Crown

☙❧

When you're trying to do God's will His way, get away from those, "If I were you people"; they're not you. And until they've walked in your shoes, they are simply giving lip service. I was on the verge of complaining to God one morning, and He quickly and quietly said to me, "no cross, no crown." After hearing Him say that, I took the hint to just shut up complaining. I began singing to the top of my lungs, and off key may I add, for at least 15 minutes.

"N o o o C r oooooooosssss, no cr o w n, I got my cross, and I'm goin get my crown." My husband said, "Oh Lord." I continued singing, "n o o o o o c r o o o s s, no c r o o w n."

Listen, if you don't have a cross to bear, you certainly won't get a crown for bearing it. Trust God with every thing. Don't just trust him with your bills; trust him with your family, career, health and all the cares that apply to you. Dying isn't easy. Staying dead is even harder. **But as it is written, Eye hath not seen, nor ear heard, neither hath entered into the heart of man, the things which God hath prepared for them that love him. (1 Corinthians 2:9 KJV)**

God has a plan for us all. Some things we go through aren't about us, nor are they because of us. No matter what comes your way, as long as God gets the glory, that should give you a sense of peace. It should give you some sort of satisfaction. There's a dying world out there, and people need to hear your story the story of how you were brought out of the Fiery Furnace and not burned, the story of how God delivered you from a Death sentence, the story of how you were left for dead, but God gave you Life, the story of how you became Drug-free, Aids-free. Tell how your sanity was restored. We all have a story to tell.

Who could benefit from your life?

Paul said, **I have fought a good fight, I have finished my course, I have kept the faith: henceforth there is laid up for me a crown of righteousness, which the Lord, the righteous judge, shall give me at that day: and not to me only, but unto all them also that love his appearing. (2 Timothy 4:7-8 KJV)** We should all bear our cross in such a way as to have the same testimony.

The apostle John says that we **overcome by the blood of the lamb and by the word of our testimony. (Revelation 12:11(a) NIV)** If you've been tested, then you have a testimony.

Finally, the Lord says, "Well Done, Thy Good and Faithful Servant. You have been faithful over a few things.

BUT,

WILL YOU DIE TO SLOTHFULNESS??????"

9 781594 676284